THE FERTILE EARTH AND THE ORDERED COSMOS

THE FERTILE EARTH AND THE ORDERED COSMOS

REFLECTIONS ON THE NEWARK EARTHWORKS AND WORLD HERITAGE

Edited by M. Elizabeth Weiser, Timothy R. W. Jordan, and Richard D. Shiels

TRILLIUM, AN IMPRINT OF
THE OHIO STATE UNIVERSITY PRESS
COLUMBUS

Trillium, an imprint of The Ohio State University Press.

Library of Congress Cataloging-in-Publication Data

Names: Weiser, M. Elizabeth, editor. | Jordan, Timothy R. W., editor. | Shiels, Richard
    D., 1947– editor.

Title: The fertile earth and the ordered cosmos : reflections on the Newark
    Earthworks and world heritage / edited by M. Elizabeth Weiser, Timothy R. W.
    Jordan, and Richard D. Shiels.

Other titles: Reflections on the Newark Earthworks and world heritage

Description: Columbus : Trillium, an imprint of The Ohio State University Press [2023]
    | Summary: "An exploration of Ohio's Newark Earthworks, the largest geometric
    earthen complex ever known, which aims to provide the general public with a
    sense of the importance of Ohio's earthworks to the world's heritage"—Provided
    by publisher.

Identifiers: LCCN 2022047039 | ISBN 9780814258705 (paperback) | ISBN
    9780814282878 (ebook)

Subjects: LCSH: Newark Earthworks (Newark, Ohio) | Mounds—Ohio—Newark. |
    Hopewell culture—Ohio. | Newark (Ohio)—Antiquities.

Classification: LCC E99.H69 F47 2023 | DDC 977.1/54—dc23/eng/20221005

LC record available at https://lccn.loc.gov/2022047039

Cover design by Nathan Putens
Text design by Juliet Williams
Type set in Azo Sans

PRINTED IN CHINA

Contents

Illustrations

Foreword: Making the Earthworks Public

RICHARD D. SHIELS

The articles in this book are part of nearly two centuries of effort to preserve and provide access to the Newark Earthworks for the education and enjoyment of all people—an effort that mirrors the centuries of preservation by Ohio's ancient Indigenous peoples. The articles, which in somewhat different forms originally appeared as individual columns in the *Newark Advocate* newspaper 2019–2022, seek to explain to the general public the history, the uniqueness, and the importance of Ohio's earthworks to the world's heritage. They bring together Native people and scholars, state officials and local residents to enlighten but also to invoke some of the love and awe that this amazing, ancient complex has inspired in so many people through the centuries.

Here are the outlines of the story.

Nearly 2,000 years ago, ancestors of today's Native people built the largest complex of geometric earthworks in the entire world within the boundaries of what is today Newark and Heath, Ohio. It was an astounding achievement which required sophisticated knowledge of geometry and astronomy as well as art and architecture. The Newark Earthworks will almost certainly be inscribed on the UNESCO World Heritage list as part of the Hopewell Ceremonial Earthworks. In spring 2022, the US Department of the Interior nominated the Newark Earthworks, Fort Ancient, and the five sites of the Hopewell Culture National Historical Park for consideration by the United Nations Educational, Scientific and Cultural Organization's (UNESCO) World Heritage Committee. They will be considered for inscription on the UNESCO World Heritage list when the Committee meets in 2023, and if inscribed their status will honor the legacy of this ancient Woodlands culture and become Ohio's most significant historical destination.

The Newark Earthworks were the largest and most precise of the earthen enclosures that ancient Hopewell-era cultures built at nearly 600 sites within the boundaries of our state: hundreds of circles, squares, combinations of circles and squares, and one other octagon-and-circle. All these enclosures are the remnants of a brilliant culture that existed here a millennium and more before Europeans arrived.

By 1900, however, nearly all these enclosures had been destroyed by settlers building towns and roads and farms and factories. Today, Newark's Great Circle and its Octagon with attached Observatory Circle are the last of the original 2,000-year-old geometric enclosures remaining fully intact, and the only places where the public might still see them and walk within them.

It was ordinary people living in Newark in the 1850s who saved the Great Circle. By that time, the site had been divided into several farms. These ordinary local people raised money, bought those farms, and saved the Great Circle from the gradual destruction that flattened so many Indigenous mounds of all kinds. They used the site as the county fairgrounds and eventually it became an amusement park, still preserving its distinctive mound-and-moat formation.

In the 1890s, civic officials initiated an effort to save the Octagon just over a mile away. That site, too, had been divided into farms by then, and these city and county leaders offered the public a plan to preserve it: purchase the Octagon and give it to the State of Ohio to be a training ground for the state militia.

It was the public, hundreds of ordinary people, who voted to raise their own taxes for the money to purchase the Octagon and prevent its destruction. Within the City of Newark, the vote was three to one. The public expected their investment would bring significant numbers of people to Newark, and that it would also preserve this astounding structure.

And so, the state militia camped and trained on the grounds of the Octagon Earthworks, again preserving the distinctive mounds. Over time the militia moved on to another site. A court gave the Octagon's public deed to the Newark Board of Trade (sometimes described as a predecessor to the Chamber of Commerce), which leased it to a group of men who built a golf course on the site in 1911. Some members of the city council protested, but a judge decided in favor of the Board of Trade. According to this judge, the Newark Board of Trade held the deed in trust for the public until the city or county could find another way to maintain the site.

By 1933, the height of the Great Depression, the Board of Trade had disbanded, and the amusement park had closed, but the lease with the local golf club—the Moundbuilders Country Club—continued. The City of Newark, meanwhile, acquired the deeds to the Great Circle as well as the Octagon, and it gave them both to the organization which today is called the Ohio History Connection (OHC), a statewide organization with a mission to spark discovery of Ohio's stories. The OHC houses the state's historic preservation office and manages more than fifty sites and museums across Ohio, including its state history museum.

The pages of the *Newark Advocate* from the early 1930s leave no doubt as to why the OHC was given the deed to both sites. They were expected to work with federal New Deal programs to remove the remnants of the amusement park from the Great Circle and then remove the greens and fairways from the Octagon. Both sites would become fully public. Maps were published in which both sites were identified as "Newark State Park," although no state park was ever officially established.

More than 230 men, enrolled in Franklin D. Roosevelt's Civilian Conservation Corps, transformed the Great Circle into what locals would call Moundbuilders' Park in the summer of 1935. The next year an engineer produced a blueprint of the Octagon without a golf course, but that plan went no further. Why? Roosevelt's New Deal declined after 1936 and funding disappeared for projects like these.

The Great Circle has been fully public since 1935, but the Octagon has not. Currently, it is officially open for tours to the public on only four "non-golfing" days during the golfing season.

It has been nearly 130 years since the public voted to raise their own taxes to purchase the Octagon, and it is approaching 100 years since the city gave the deed to the OHC with the understanding that the OHC would make it public.

Today the OHC is leading the effort to win inscription on the UNESCO World Heritage list, which will bring visitors to Ohio and our community from all around the globe. They are acting with the Ohio Attorney General's Office to find a mutually agreeable buyout of the Moundbuilders Country Club's lease and make the site fully accessible to the public.

It seems that the Newark Earthworks will finally become once again what by all indications their builders must have intended: a site of awe for visitors from across the known world.

FIGURE 1.1. The gateway of the Great Circle in the early spring. Photo by Timothy E. Black.

PART I

What Are the Newark Earthworks?

Over the 2,000 years of their existence, the Newark Earthworks have served many purposes: gathering place, ceremonial site, fairground, army encampment, golf course, park. Even as some of these purposes now seem strange to us, all of them for a period preserved the Great Circle and the Octagon. The question of what is best for the sites is one we should continue to ask, and our answers should take a broad view of the whole complex's scale and history.

A Shawnee Perspective

GLENNA J. WALLACE

I wore many hats during my forty years at Crowder College, from instructor to department chair, division head, interim academic dean and director of international travel, where I led trips to more than seventy countries. In those capacities, I made numerous presentations. For two years I traveled the Chautauqua circuit performing in Lewis and Clark Bicentennial productions representing the Shawnee people. For three years I researched Shawnees and Ohio, our homelands. But not once in my research did I find mention of the Newark Earthworks. I encountered them accidentally.

In May 2007 I came to The Ohio State University to hear John Sugden, acclaimed English biographer of both Blue Jacket and Tecumseh, famous Shawnee warriors. The next day Newark Earthworks Center professors took Sugden to the Octagon Earthworks. I went along because of Sugden, not because of the Newark Earthworks.

Imagine my shock and total disbelief when I saw this amazing array of earthen walls, as impressive as any World Heritage Site I had ever seen. It was surreal. How could this be? My people lived here in Ohio for 300 years. I had read everything I could about them, but not once had I heard about the Newark Earthworks. I was stunned by what I saw.

There before me lay an extensive series of hills or walls—in short, earthworks—built by Native Americans nearly 2,000 years ago with a mathematical complexity that is mind-boggling. How these people could conceive and construct this massive earthen architecture is as astounding as the Egyptians constructing the Pyramids or the Chinese building the Great Wall.

What I saw is both beautiful and massive: earthen walls 621 feet long enclose an octagon covering forty-one acres connected to a perfect circle enclosing another twenty acres. What is more, these walls align with an 18.6-year lunar cycle. The earthworks are miraculous. Why have so many others never heard of nor experienced them?

The reason is the Octagon has been leased to a private country club and covered by a golf course. The day I was there a tournament was underway. Instead of welcoming us, cart drivers shouted, "Get back. You're in the way."

I could not believe it. My ancestors treasured these mounds. They were sacred. No, they did not build them, but they loved them, protected them, revered them. I experienced the beauty, the awe that they inspire, but I was not permitted to walk on the sacred grounds of my people. I could not even approach, much less touch these precious earthworks, earthworks that are every bit as impressive as World Heritage Sites like the Pyramids, Great Wall, Stonehenge, the Acropolis. Built in Ohio by American Indians, these earthworks remain unknown to most of the world.

At first I was in awe, proud of what my ancestors had constructed. Then I became angry, anguished, distraught. Golfing is an excellent sport, and there are other golf courses. But these sacred mounds can't be moved, replicated or experienced elsewhere. There is not another place in the world like the Newark Earthworks. They need to be shared and experienced on a daily basis by masses of people.

That day I made a commitment to learn all I could about the Newark Earthworks, to teach about them, to preserve them. I continue to be amazed, awestruck, disappointed, hurt, and angry. But there is hope. Join me in the effort to inscribe the Newark Earthworks on the United Nations Educational, Scientific and Cultural Organization (UNESCO) World Heritage List.

FIGURE 1.2. The Octagon Earthworks with its attached Observatory Circle. Photo by Timothy E. Black.

The Mystery in Our Midst

AARON KEIRNS

I have been visiting the Newark Earthworks for over fifty years, and each time I walk around them I am amazed all over again. The more I learn about these ancient mounds, the more mysterious they seem.

Anyone who has spent much time driving around Newark is probably familiar with the Great Circle Earthworks on South 21st Street and the Octagon Earthworks at Moundbuilders Country Club along North 30th Street. It's easy to forget that these two spectacular earthworks are only remnants of a much larger group of interconnected mounds that once existed here.

The Great Circle and Octagon mounds lie approximately one mile apart. Today, separated by an urban landscape, they seem like unrelated sites. But originally, they were connected to each other and to several other equally impressive mounds via parallel earthen walls that formed wide avenues. These mounds included a large square enclosure, smaller circular enclosures, and a huge ellipse surrounding several burial mounds.

Much of these mounds are now gone, flattened and paved over during the building of the city. The original group of earthworks covered about four square miles or approximately 2,500 acres in what is now southwest Newark. This is thought to be the largest complex of interconnected geometric earthworks ever built by prehistoric peoples anywhere on the planet.

Although the enormous scale of this ancient site is truly amazing, the size and precision of the giant earthen shapes that comprised it are even more so. The Great Circle, for example, is 1,200 feet in diameter. The Octagon encloses forty-one acres. The Square was about the size of nine city blocks. Each of these shapes was extremely precise—an amazing feat considering that they are estimated to have been built around 2,000 years ago.

There's more. The Octagon Earthworks was designed as a lunar calendar. Its walls perfectly align with specific points on the horizon that mark a complicated cycle of moon risings and settings that takes 18.6 years to complete.

Any one of these facts would be incredible all by itself. Together, they reveal an ancient past that presents as many questions as answers. It's impossible not to wonder about the ancestral Native people who built these enigmatic structures. What motivated them to spend so much time and effort to create gigantic geometric shapes on the landscape? How were they able to achieve the sophisticated geometrical measurements and astronomical alignments built into the mounds? How did they organize and manage the labor force needed to dig and carry millions of basket-loads of earth? These are only a few of the many mysteries associated with the Newark Earthworks.

Hard to Describe but Awesome to Experience

BRAD LEPPER

When you look at a map of Ohio showing the locations of the largest earthen enclosures built by the Indigenous American Hopewell culture between about AD 1 and 400, the Newark Earthworks stand out. Most of these extraordinary sites are in Ross County in and around Chillicothe, which must have been ground zero for what the late N'omi Greber referred to as the Hopewell explosion. The five amazing earthworks that make up Hopewell Culture National Historical Park are among these.

Other monumental Hopewell earthworks are found along the Ohio River and the major rivers in southern Ohio that flow into the Ohio. These include the sprawling Fort Ancient Earthworks, perched on a bluff overlooking the Little Miami River in Warren County.

The Newark Earthworks stand out as the most northern expression of this Indigenous explosion of art, architecture, and ceremony. While they stand isolated on the northernmost edge of what has been called the Hopewell Core, they are the largest and most complicated grouping of geometric earthworks in the Hopewell world. Ephraim Squier and Edwin Davis, who published maps and descriptions of the major Hopewell earthworks in the very first volume of the Smithsonian Institution's *Contributions to Knowledge* series, wrote that they were so complicated "it is impossible to give anything like a comprehensible description of them."

Much of the Newark Earthworks has been lost to farm fields, roads, houses, and shops. Two magnificent parts have, however, been pre-served: the Great Circle and the Octagon Earthworks. In addition, a tiny remnant of a square enclosure is preserved at the Wright Earthworks.

Although the Newark Earthworks appears to be isolated on the Hopewell frontier, it exhibits clear and convincing connections to the more southerly Hopewell earthworks. For example, the large circle connected by a parallel-walled avenue to the Octagon at Newark has the same diameter as the circles at the Hopeton and High Bank Works in Ross County. In addition, Newark's Wright Square has the same area as the square enclosure at the Hopeton Earthworks.

Newark's Octagon Earthworks incorporates alignments to the points on the eastern horizon that mark the maximum northern and maximum southern risings of the moon. These same alignments are built into the High Bank Works and the Fort Ancient Earthworks.

These examples show that Hopewell earthworks builders in Newark shared with their southern cousins the same sophisticated understanding of geometry and astronomy, as well as of measurement, surveying, and of which soils were the best to use for building enduring earthen walls.

I also think that the Newark Earthworks were linked directly to the Hopewell Core by a ceremonial highway defined by a set of remarkably straight, parallel earthen walls that extended from the southeastern corner of Newark's Octagon on a compass bearing that points directly to the center of modern Chillicothe. Whether this Great Hopewell Road reached that far has not yet been determined, but it is similar to ancient roads that were as long or even longer, built by the Ancestral Puebloans at Chaco Canyon in New Mexico and by the ancient Maya civilization.

The Newark Earthworks, the Fort Ancient Earthworks, and the earthworks at Hopewell Culture National Historical Park have been combined into the Hopewell Ceremonial Earthworks for nomination to the UNESCO World Heritage List. Each site has its own remarkable story to tell, but together they teach us about ancient Indigenous societies that came together, without an authoritarian leader to forcibly unite them, to create not just a number of huge earthen cathedrals but a vast and interconnected ceremonial landscape.

The remnants of that landscape preserved across southern and central Ohio, along with an understanding of how it was created, retain the power to inspire us.

FIGURE 1.3. View of multiple mounds at the Octagon. Photo by Brad Lepper.

A Traveling Architect's View

JOHN E. HANCOCK

In my line of work, I need to know about important architectural monuments around the world.

As an architectural historian, I did a lot of traveling to Europe and saw many World Heritage Sites. Besides all the cultural landmarks, there was much to be savored in the overall tourist experience: historic towns, small family-run inns, local cuisine, and scenic byways—a rich immersion in the spirit of place. In the coming years, as Newark and southern Ohio embrace their World Heritage opportunity, we will have the opportunity to offer much to the many cultural heritage travelers who will visit us from around the world to experience our spectacular earthworks.

I've taught architecture and its history at the University of Cincinnati for forty years. I'd already been there half that time, teaching my students about the famous places in Greece, Rome, and medieval Europe, before I discovered the monumental ancient works right here in Ohio that are, in their own way, just as spectacular and fascinating.

Though I had been to a lot of places and seen a lot of wonderful cultural sites, nothing quite prepared me for my first experience of Ancient Newark. Standing beside the walls of the Octagon, my mouth fell open: "I had no idea!" Such utter astonishment, I've since learned, is a frequent response.

The brilliance of Ohio's ancient Indigenous peoples has been hidden from most of us for decades. In the 1800s, white folks couldn't believe Indians had built anything so sophisticated, and so they conjured theories of a "lost race" of moundbuilders. Since then, as most of the earthworks were being destroyed, we generally came to assume our mid-America landscapes had no deep history at all before the pioneers cleared the forests and built the canals.

So, what does this lost brilliance consist of? What do the earthworks tell us? As an architectural educator, I am intrigued by the sites' precision of form, their almost incomprehensible scale, and their uncanny beauty. Like all great architectural monuments, they don't just tell us stories from the past, they teach us in the present; they offer new ways of understanding our world—the earth, the sky, and our fellow humans.

When my architect friends from around the world visit, we often tour the earthworks (also Fort Ancient, Serpent Mound, and Mound City), and that same astonishment is reflected anew: they had no idea! And there's a reason I always save Newark's Great Circle and Octagon for last: their scope, beauty, and precision are the most dazzling of all.

After twenty years of immersion in this topic, producing exhibits and the Ancient Ohio Trail (ancientohiotrail.org), I am honored to be helping prepare these places (Newark's Octagon and Great Circle, plus six others) for inscription as UNESCO World Heritage Sites. This will confer upon them the global recognition they and their builders deserve: as works of creative genius, products of a brilliant culture, and places of eternal importance to all of humanity.

FIGURE 1.4. The Great Circle. Photo by Timothy E. Black.

Earthworks Terminology

RICHARD D. SHIELS

How do we talk about the earthworks? Our terminology can be confusing.

Take the term *Hopewell culture*. There never were Indigenous people who called themselves *Hopewell*. While there is no doubt that our earthworks were built by ancestors of today's Native people, we simply do not know which nations or tribes might be descended from the people who built these mounds. Bret Ruby, archaeologist at the Hopewell Culture National Historic Park, says he thinks of Hopewell as a religious movement or an era of time when this religious movement held sway in eastern North America.

Archaeologists came up with the term *Hopewell culture* in the nineteenth century when they decided that geometric earthworks sites, built across a wide spectrum of America between 100 BCE and 500 CE, were evidence of a widespread culture. The earthworks they called Hopewell were different from those they assigned to the Adena culture (which was older) and the Mississippian culture (which was younger). The key word here is *culture,* a key concept in archaeology.

But why did they select these names?

They chose the term *Adena* because the first earthworks they placed in this category were on Thomas Worthington's estate, which he had named Adena. The term *Mississippian* was chosen because the most impressive site is on the Mississippi River. So, why choose *Hopewell*? One of the most impressive sites in this group was on a farm owned by Civil War veteran Mordecai Hopewell.

The terms *mounds* and *earthworks* also deserve consideration. Beginning about 1830, a narrative we now call "the moundbuilders myth" spread across the country. This false narrative denied the obvious fact that the earthworks had been built by Native ancestors. The moundbuilders myth posited that an unknown race of white people built the mounds but later died out for unknown reasons. In that same decade, when the federal government began removing American Indians from Ohio and other states and resettling them in what would become Oklahoma, the public was ready to believe that Indians were not smart enough to have built these monumental structures throughout the lands they were being forced to leave. The Smithsonian put to rest the moundbuilders myth in the 1890s, with research which concluded that the mounds were in fact built by ancestral Indigenous people. Today the experts are more likely to use the term *earthworks* rather than *mounds*, perhaps to avoid giving any credence to the moundbuilders myth.

So, perhaps the single most important thing to say about our earthworks is that they were built by ancestors of today's Indigenous people.

The Greatness of the Great Circle

TIMOTHY R. W. JORDAN

The Great Circle.

We talk a lot about greatness, but what do we mean by *great*?

In my work as both an interpreter and a writing instructor, tangibles and intangibles are important. Tangibles are things that can be measured or understood through the senses. Intangibles are value statements that, while important, are best understood when paired with tangibles. *Greatness* is an intangible.

So, again, what do we mean by *great*?

With the Great Circle, size certainly comes into play. Encompassing an area of thirty acres and with a diameter of 1,200 feet, it is huge, tremendous (two other intangibles). Put differently, four football fields would fit end-to-end across it. The Great Pyramid of Giza could sit inside it.

Greatness can be more than size. It can include vision.

The Great Circle is just one of four interconnected sites that once made up the Newark Earthworks. The Octagon and its attached Observatory Circle also still stand, but they were connected by walkways to a square and an ellipse. The more than four square miles that these shapes and walkways covered are impressive enough, but an underlying use of geometry further unifies Newark's sites. For one example, the distance between the centers of the Observatory and Great Circles equals exactly six times the 1,054-foot diameter of Observatory Circle. The perimeter of the Wright Square and the circumference of the Great Circle are equal. All parts of the Newark Earthworks are pulled together on both material and geometric levels into a unified statement.

Greatness can include artistry.

There is beauty in the earthworks' use of geometry, but their architecture is also stunning. Standing inside the Great Circle and looking back toward its gateway, the twelve-foot sides of its opening are noticeably the high-points of the wall. Both sides quickly taper down and level off, so an artificial horizon encompasses most of the site's thirty acres. We don't know if this horizon relates to any sort of celestial alignment, as we see with a number of other earthworks sites, but it is a remarkable aesthetic. Below this level wall is the Great Circle's inner moat, which we speculate held water. The resulting juxtaposition of water, earth, and sky overlaps with the rich imagery and themes of much Native mythology, which envisions the earth brought into being between the sky world above and the watery world beneath.

Greatness can include community.

The scale, geometrical knowledge, architectural aesthetic, and apparent symbolism of the Great Circle all point toward the deep investment of many people to achieve such end results. Archaeologists also point to this effort being one that was peaceful, noting that human remains from burials of this time period show few signs of traumatic injuries—no spearpoints embedded in rib cages or crushed skulls, the kinds of injuries that would point to warfare and violence.

These dimensions of ancient Indigenous people's greatness go beyond the Great Circle.

The Octagon with its eight lunar alignments in an 18.6-year cycle is magnificent. So is Fort Ancient, a 3.5-mile hilltop enclosure in Oregonia that incorporates solar alignments. So too are the sites that make up Hopewell Culture National Historical Park in Chillicothe, a sampling of five of the dozens of earthworks that once stood along twelve miles of the Scioto River.

Together, these eight earthworks sites across three communities make up the Hopewell Ceremonial Earthworks nomination for the World Heritage List. Our communities' opportunity to bring these sites onto the international stage is a chance to join today's Indigenous peoples in celebrating the achievements of their ancestors, Ohio's ancient people.

That too would be great.

FIGURE 2.1. Digital recreation of the maximum northern moonrise at the Octagon. This rendering emphasizes the moon's ascent along the site's main axis. Image by John E. Hancock.

PART II

Uniting Earth and Sky

The decision of ancient Native people to build the Newark Earthworks in what is now called Licking County was deliberate and well-planned. The scale and architecture of these sites make them monuments unto themselves, but the builders also made the earthworks celebrations of the bounty of the landscape from which they grew. Furthermore, as the earthworks reach toward the sky, they connect the matter of this world into a grand cosmology. Although we can at best only infer some of the builders' beliefs, the sophistication and depth of these beliefs are evident in the lunar alignments and geometry that were harnessed in their expression.

Exciting Times

JOHN N. LOW

Growing up in southwest Michigan and northwest Indiana among the Pokagon Band of Potawatomi Indians, I was fortunate to be able to participate in the social and spiritual life of that community. I have always known about "Indian Mounds." My ancestors were mound builders too, and I was taught stories at an early age about our connections to them.

I also knew about such places as Cahokia, the incredible Mississippian Indigenous city and mounds near St. Louis. However, until coming to a conference at The Ohio State University at Newark in 2005 as a graduate student, I never knew about the Newark Earthworks. I was amazed at the size and beauty of the Great Circle and the Octagon and impressed by the complex lunar observatory that is at least one of the functions of the Octagon. Even though much of the original earthworks complex was lost as Newark grew as a city, I was impressed that Ohioans had had the foresight to preserve these two special places. I was especially excited when I was hired in 2012 to teach at Ohio State and return to these incredible earthworks.

As I tell my students, the Newark Earthworks were likely a ceremonial space. They reflect sophisticated knowledge of geometry and astronomy and are tangible evidence that disrupts the stereotype of Indians as nomadic savages moving about the woods. These were very smart people who farmed, hunted, and lived semi-sedentary lives in balance with their surroundings.

The preference of many peoples around the world is to build their monuments out of stone. Stone seems to impress a lot of people. And they like them tall, the taller the better! We need to remember that the horizontal was apparently equally important to those who built the Earthworks. If the Octagon stood on its side, its vertical reach would be taller than the Pyramids at Giza. The earthworks are also made of dirt. We use *dirt* as a pejorative—something "dirty" to be avoided. But the builders here used the material most sacred to them: earth, Mother Earth. I remember when Pokagon Potawatomi elders took a bus trip to visit the Newark Earthworks in 2012. Many of them told me, both during their visit and after, how affected they were by the spaces. Indigenous peoples all over the United States have a connection to these Earthworks. They retain a meaning and power that we are only beginning to access.

As a center for The Ohio State University, the small but passionate team at the Newark Earthworks Center has a unique opportunity to promote scholarly engagement and research as well as to contribute to the efforts of World Heritage Ohio to have the Hopewell Ceremonial Earthworks designated a UNESCO World Heritage Site. The residents of Newark and Ohio deserve to be proud of the treasures they have here. These are exciting times.

Licking County's Ancient Treasures

BILL WEAVER

I love Licking County. I grew up here, raised my children here, and several of them are still here, raising their children in Licking County schools.

There is a great deal to love: the people, of course; the churches and schools; the spring flowers and fall colors and much more. As the years have gone by, however, I have come to increasingly treasure our history—our amazing, ancient history. People have been coming to Licking County for thousands of years.

I grew up only a few blocks from the Great Circle and Octagon earthworks. It was common for my family to have picnics at the Great Circle. In 1970 I became the principal of Toboso Elementary School, which is next to Black Hand Gorge. Knowing very little about the area, I was guided by science teacher Twyla Hessin. I learned that Native people traveling on the river had used the gorge as a transportation route just as later European settlers did with the railroad (and now hiking/biking trail). I realized the Gorge's amazing potential and the educational value it held for our students. We adapted many areas of our curriculum around the elements of what came to be a State Nature Preserve. While I was at Toboso, we gave guided tours for hundreds of visiting students over twenty years' time. Fascinating to all was the name Black Hand, coming from the name of a petroglyph on the stone cliff called Council Rock. Twice the size of a human hand, it was believed to have pointed Native people to the flint quarries six miles to the south. The flint debitage littering the sandstone at Black Hand Gorge is proof of its connection to Flint Ridge.

Today I am an officer of the Licking Valley Heritage Society, which partners with the Ohio History Connection to manage Flint Ridge Ancient Quarries and Nature Preserve. This park includes more than *1,000* flint quarries. Flint Ridge flint is the most unique and beautiful flint in the world. It has provided tools such as knives, scrapers, drill bits, and arrowheads for Native people for tens of thousands of years. No doubt ancient people used these tools to harvest deer—even today the salt licks of *Licking* County draw more deer than those in any of the other eighty-eight counties of Ohio. Well-fed and strong, then, people who lived during the Hopewell era built the largest geometric earthworks in the world eleven miles from Flint Ridge 2,000 years ago.

Many groups and individuals take advantage of the proximity of these three beautiful and historic sites to visit them much as the ancients did eons ago. The prolific trade of the colorful flint, evidenced by finding our flint artifacts across the country, has contributed to our knowledge of the significance of the area, making it all the more worthy of World Heritage designation. It is clear to me that Licking Countians have a responsibility to preserve these sites and share them with the world.

FIGURE 2.2. (*facing*) Time-lapse photo of the maximum northern moonrise through the Octagon's passageway from Observatory Circle. Because of the earth's rotation, the moon tracks at a diagonal from its alignment point on the horizon. Photo by Timothy E. Black.

Nature and the Newark Earthworks

JIM WILLIAMS

Two thousand and more years ago, the area we call Ohio was covered from top to bottom with a dense ancient forest. It has been said that a squirrel could get from Lake Erie to the Ohio River without touching the ground. Clever hunter-gatherers hunted mastodons, and later deer, long before the Newark Earthworks were built.

They noticed that deer loved to congregate in grassy clearings to feed, and it was in these areas where it was easier to hunt. Probably using stone axes and fire, they cleared the forest from the area just south of Racoon Creek and west of the South Fork of the Licking River to create a human-made hunting ground. Soil sample analysis now confirms that there were no trees in the area which we call the Newark Earthworks for hundreds of years before these great geometric mounds were built.

These observant folks also had long known that the area where the Earthworks would later be was built was on a plateau located above the floodplain. If you are going to construct something of dirt, you don't want your efforts washed away in a spring flood. These ancient folks also had a plan to keep their construction well preserved: they allowed native grasses to grow on the mounds and grounds surrounding the area. Grass is nature's best soil erosion preventer.

But why here? For the answer to that, we need only look at the geography already before the earthworks builders' eyes.

The arrangement of the natural physical features of the area already aligns with the lunar cycle. These alignments are possible because several hills are located where they are. The people noticed that the moonset moved back and forth in a dramatic fashion between two major valleys, as viewed from the highest elevation in the Newark area.

And why the octagonal shape?

The people had long been experimenting with geometric shapes. They discovered that an octagonal design, slightly distorted from the ideal, made the lunar alignments they were concerned about even more precise.

I am sure this discovery of the close connection between geometric symmetry and the movements of the moon galvanized interest in both geometry and astronomy during that time.

The stage was set. The grounds were clear of trees. The canvas was blank. It was ready-made to be reshaped. All it took was a vision to inspire, the will to make it happen, and an energized people willing to devote their blood, sweat, and tears to a project bigger than themselves and their own generation.

Archaeologist Brad Lepper has described the process of moving 7,000,000 cubic feet of earth by hand: "They were built with pointed digging sticks and perhaps hoes or picks, made with a deer shoulder blade and hafted onto a stick—simple tools. The Hopewell people used this to dig pits in the ground and then fill the earth . . . in baskets and carry those baskets one at a time to mound them one after another."

The earthworks throughout the Hopewell sphere of influence are a testimony to how a people reshaped nature while also revering it. So, when you visit the Newark Earthworks, admire the work of reshaping nature which ancient people performed 2,000 and more years ago.

How We Found the Lunar Alignments at the Octagon

RAY HIVELY AND ROBERT HORN

We have said we first came to the Newark Earthworks to settle a bet, but that is the husk of the story.

In the summer of 1974 Ray Hively was a newly minted astrophysicist. Bob Horn, a philosopher, was on sabbatical leave in Denmark. Our dean at Earlham College cleverly sandwiched us into an intensive year-long course in the history of cosmology. Never having met, we grumbled.

At the time, the British site of Stonehenge was at the center of a controversy around the claim that Stonehenge and other related "megalithic" (large stone) sites in Europe and the Mediterranean pointed out key stages (standstills) in the travel of the rising/setting sun and moon on the horizon. Perhaps it was a ritual calendar, went the argument: two stones or figures in line could be utilized as a solar or lunar pointer. We were skeptical. There was then no thorough map of Stonehenge, and little knowledge of its archaeology or history. How could we enable our students to understand the long-term work required, in many disciplines, before such a claim could be decided?

We helped them learn elementary mapping. We got permission to map a small section of Fort Ancient, a Hopewell-era site sixty miles from Earlham. They soon learned a lot about the difficulty of mapping a site with (in 1974) no adequate archaeological and historical record. Lacking that history, Ray bet our class that he could claim any site we might choose was a solar observatory simply by focusing on random alignments which were always likely to be present in a complex structure.

Bob suggested we go to Newark. Acquainted with the site, he guessed two things we later found to be true:

1. The Newark Octagon is well documented. It is essentially what it was 1800 years ago.
2. The Newark Octagon is a geometrically regular construction.

We set out to resurvey the Newark Octagon, occasionally competing with golfers for access. Our completed survey and archival study, three summers later, agreed substantially with the Smithsonian Institution's survey from 1887. So, we looked for the sun.

When we chose pointers or sightlines defined by the geometry of the Octagon, we could find no alignments to the sun at the solstices. Ray quipped that perhaps there was a cult of solar avoidance. But the complete lack of even random solar alignments was itself improbable, suggesting the site might be aligned to something else: perhaps the moon.

At Stonehenge and a few other sites in Britain and Mexico, some had claimed alignments to the moon. We thought deliberate lunar alignments unlikely at Newark. In contrast to the sun's yearly cycle, the complete lunar cycle lasts 18.6 years, difficult to track under the best conditions. In central Ohio, the moon on the horizon is very often veiled by clouds.

However, at the Newark Octagon where we had found no alignments to the sun, we found five alignments to the moon, one on the symmetry axis of the Observatory Circle and Octagon and four on the Octagon walls. Was it plausible that the builders not only tracked the moon accurately in this difficult environment, but that they also ignored the more accessible sun? The puzzle ignited our research.

After examining other geometric figures surrounding the Newark Earthworks and their relationship to the local topography, we found over a dozen accurate alignments to the lunar standstills. We were also to find that lunar alignments discovered at the Newark Octagon predicted major design features of Newark and other Ohio Hopewell-era earthworks.

Eventually we found the sun as well, first at High Bank, south of Chillicothe, later at other Ohio Hopewell-era sites, and years later at Newark itself, where four solstice locations in the hills surrounding Cherry Valley anchor the whole lunar array in the earthworks below.

Ray was sufficiently impressed with the solstice sunrise at Newark that he brought his bride to Newark to spend their wedding night and watch the solstice sunrise the following morning over the Octagon Earthworks. On their honeymoon years earlier, Bob had taken his bride to Mound City.

We came to Newark forty-six years ago to extend field work in a faculty–student project and incidentally to settle a bet. Baffling our expectations, the genius of the Indigenous builders, the magnificence of their creation, and the generosity of the community working to understand them hold us there still.

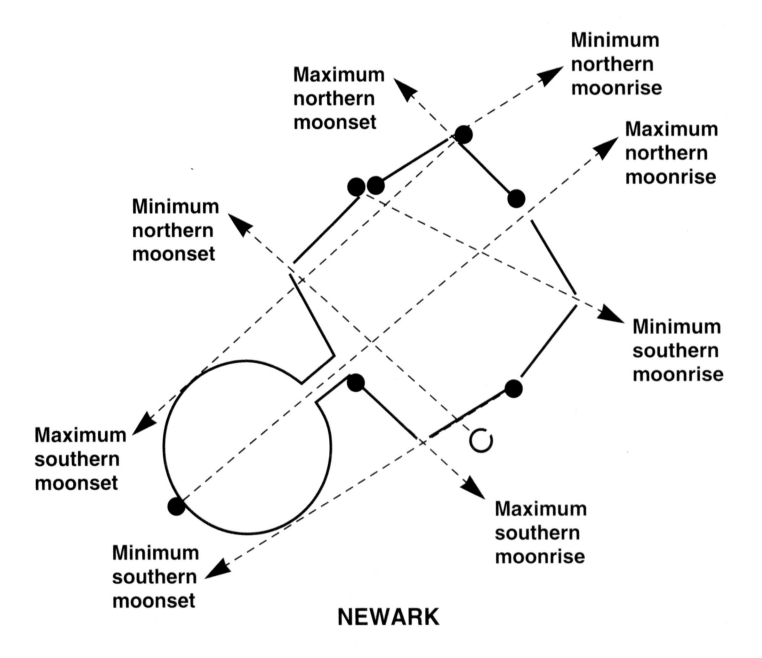

Maximum northern moonset

Minimum northern moonrise

Maximum northern moonrise

Minimum northern moonset

Minimum southern moonrise

Maximum southern moonset

Maximum southern moonrise

Minimum southern moonset

NEWARK

FIGURE 2.3. Diagram showing the angles for viewing each of the eight lunar risings and settings at Newark's Octagon. Used with permission from the Ohio History Connection.

Just How Does the Octagon Align with the Moon?

RICHARD D. SHIELS

Many readers know that the Octagon Earthworks was built to align with the movements of the moon. Fewer know just how that works.

We are talking about places on the horizon where the moon rises or sets: the *maximum northern, maximum southern, minimum northern,* and *minimum southern* moonrises and corresponding moonsets. On each of these eight occasions the moon seems to change directions in the sky. Let me explain it by imagining how ancient people might have figured it out.

Imagine that you are an Indigenous person living 2,000 years ago. Every night you see the moon rising and setting, and like any careful watcher of the world around you, you notice that it doesn't do this in the same place every night. You start to observe closely, recording your observations.

Let's say you begin your observations on the day of the month that the moon rises at its northernmost point on the eastern horizon. Each night for the next fourteen nights or so (actually exactly half of 29.5 nights) you watch it rise a little bit further south. Then it spends the other half of those 29.5 nights retracing its path back to the northernmost point. We have a name for this 29.5-day period: we call it a lunar month.

You continue your observations for a second, third, fourth month, and you start to notice that, even though the moon retraces its path on the horizon north and south over the months, it doesn't return to the exact same points. You see that, month by month, it rises (and sets) a little bit further to the north, and a little bit further to the south, like an angle getting wider.

Eventually its path reaches the *maximum northern* and *maximum southern* points of rising on the horizon—and then it starts to contract again. In fact, 9.3 years later—after another 112 months of nightly observations—you observe its rising points on the horizon reach the *minimum northern* and *minimum southern* points. And then its path starts to expand again.

You (or your descendants) have now made careful observations of the moon for 18.6 years, nearly 7000 nightly observations. But was this a one-time phenomenon? It's time to make observations for another 18.6 years, to be sure.

That is what we need to know about the moon. Here is what we need to know about the Octagon. It is clear that ancient people knew about the alignments they built so carefully into its structure 2,000 years ago. Probably they had observed and recorded the moon's journey not merely through one cycle but through several—generations of observations to determine that it was consistent, and that they could build a giant complex that would accurately mark its path.

Perhaps our most impressive rediscovery is that the maximum northern rise point perfectly bisects the center of the Octagon, and that extending its path through the passage connecting the octagon to its circle brings us to what we today call the Observatory Mound in its interior. But we have also rediscovered that the walls of the Octagon align with four of the other seven moonrises or sets—evidence of those decades of long-ago careful observation.

How impressive is that?

The Rhythm of the Moon Written on the Land

MIKE MICKELSON

March 7, 2025, marks the next lunar standstill. "So what?" you say. For eons humans have watched the sky and appreciated the movements of wandering celestial bodies—sun, moon, planets, and comets—but direct public observation is less common in modern times.

Apart from professional and amateur astronomers, and the general public when a highly publicized eclipse or comet is imminent, most people pay little attention to the goings-on in the sky. An exception that brought out literally millions was the August 21, 2017, Great American Solar Eclipse, viewable across a large swath of the US. By some reports over 215 million American adults viewed this once-in-a-lifetime solar eclipse, more than watched the last Super Bowl. Infrequent events such as lunar standstills are less known and bring out fewer of us.

Most of us, however, are aware of solar standstills. You know, the winter and summer solstices. For many days, the sun appears to rise and set at nearly the same location on the horizon. I calculated that in 2020, the winter solstice lasted for around twenty-seven days. These cycles are annual. But what about lunar standstills, called *lunistices* by some astronomers, which occur on complex schedules? Actually, two cycles are woven together: a monthly one that occurs every 29.5 days and another that repeats on an 18.6-year cycle. The monthly rhythm occurs within the longer one. How exactly does that work?

Each month as we watch the rising and setting of the moon, we can see that it marches daily from most northerly rise and set points on the horizon to most southerly ones, and then returns to the north to repeat the cycle in 29.5 days. The longer cycle repeats this movement on a larger scale every 18.6 years.

The people who designed and constructed the Newark Octagon Earthworks encoded the major lunar standstill as well as a so-called minor standstill on the landscape in the forms of these elaborate earthworks. The genius of these folks brought together ancient knowledge of the sky, a design reflecting the cosmos, and the organization of a monumental effort for reasons we don't completely understand. This remarkable effort will be recognized again in the observations of this 18.6-year cyclical event in March of 2025 and the months surrounding. It is a standstill, so it will recur for many months before and after the technical astronomical date. The moon's travels through space and time are encoded in the Newark Octagon.

FIGURE 2.4. (*facing*) Time-lapse photo showing how the moon's southern progression along the horizon turns the Octagon's southernmost wall into a sightline for viewing the minimum northern moonrise. Photo by Timothy E. Black.

The Rest of the Story

BRAD LEPPER

Most people think of the Newark Earthworks as two separate parks—the Great Circle in Heath and the Octagon Earthworks in Newark. There is another park, the Wright Earthworks, a small remnant of a large square enclosure along with a short piece of one of originally two parallel walls that framed an avenue connecting the square with a giant, now obliterated, elliptical enclosure in which there were twelve burial mounds.

When you look at a map of the entire Newark Earthworks it may not, at first glance, appear to be anything more than a conglomeration of separate earthworks haphazardly connected to one another by parallel-walled avenues. Most archaeologists probably think the Newark Earthworks were built just that way—a piece at a time over the course of a century or more. But the evidence for a unified composition with subtle (and some not-so-subtle) connections between each of the individual enclosures suggests to me a different possibility: that some revered religious leader, the equivalent of a Buddha or a Moses, designed the whole thing and then inspired thousands of people to come to the Raccoon Creek valley to participate in the creation of a wonder of the world.

Consider some of those connections. The circumference of the Great Circle is equal to the perimeter of the Wright Square. The area of the large circle at the Octagon Earthworks is equal to the area of the Wright Square. In fact, each of the separate earthworks has a geometrical connection to one or more of the other earthworks.

Consider as well that each of the large earthworks is unique. There was an octagon, a square, and an ellipse. There are two large circles, but they are different. The Great Circle has an interior ditch that held water. The circle connected to the octagon does not. In addition, the Octagon Earthworks is the only enclosure that incorporates alignments to all eight points on the horizon that mark the entire 18.6-year-long cycle of moonrises and sets.

I think this means that each enclosure was built for a separate but complementary purpose: something like the gears and connecting rods of a machine. Pilgrims would enter the earthworks along one of the parallel-walled avenues and then move in a prescribed sequence from one enclosure to the next, performing ceremonies specific to each.

If I'm right, then the Indigenous Hopewell-era builders of the Newark Earthworks conceived of the site as one massive ceremonial machine. It was linked to the heavens by the Octagon's alignments to the moon and to the powers of the watery World Below by three parallel-walled avenues that led to each of the surrounding streams.

What was this machine built to do?

We may never know, but according to the late Vine Deloria Jr., a member of the Standing Rock Sioux nation, Indigenous architecture often "represented and reproduced" the larger cosmos so that "people did not feel alone. They participated in cosmic rhythms."

Maybe that's enough of an answer.

FIGURE 3.1. (*facing*) View from Observatory Circle of the passage connecting back to the Octagon. Photo by Brad Lepper.

PART III

What Is World Heritage?

World Heritage status is granted through the United Nations Educational, Scientific and Cultural Organization (UNESCO). This designation marks its member sites as being of such cultural significance or natural beauty that they should be noted and protected for all of humanity. World Heritage Sites bring people together to contemplate the past, the present, and the future. As part of the Hopewell Ceremonial Earthworks nomination, the Newark Earthworks ask us to reconsider our understandings of ancient Indigenous peoples and to celebrate their achievements.

Rising to the Occasion

STACEY HALFMOON

In a sense, the Hopewell Ceremonial Earthworks UNESCO World Heritage nomination (including the Newark Earthworks) is a traditional lands acknowledgement. It acknowledges the people who are indigenous to this region. It also calls attention to the fact that the ancestors of modern American Indian people have been living here for well over 12,000 years, over 500 generations.

In my experience, history is personal for American Indian people, even ancient history. Who I am today as a woman, a mother, a Tribal citizen is inextricably linked to my family, my grandparents, my great-grandparents, my ancient ancestors, and, beyond that, to all Native relations.

The past, the (hi)stories, and the ancestors are ever-present. Although part of that history is tragic—including forced removals, geographical disconnect from homelands and burial grounds, disease and colonization—our ancestors persisted. We see evidence of their lives, are blessed by their wisdom, and remember their accomplishments. Their sacrifices were big-hearted and visionary; they included considering what is best for their people and even for their yet unborn great-great-great-grandchildren.

Because of their strength and wisdom, many of our sacred places still exist. Despite any disconnect of time or place to these sites, there is an inherited reverence for these places—especially places such as the earthworks.

Earthworks are a living testament to the intelligence of Indigenous ancestors and their understanding of the world around them. They knew this land—its rivers, its hills, its animals, its cycles, its skies, its seasons, its sunsets and moonrises. Our ancestors gathered in these places and created these monumental spaces by working together. The world will enjoy visiting and seeking to understand the *why* of these great earthworks.

There is a growing movement towards community-engaged scholarship wherein scholars, both Native and non-Native, more directly explore how they might work together on projects that might benefit Indigenous communities. For example, The Ohio State University has led significant research efforts over the last decade, inviting Tribal leaders, Tribal citizens, artists, and others to visit the earthworks in Newark and share their thoughts about them.

When visiting, I find myself pondering what ceremonies were held, what foods were prepared, what songs were sung. As Native people who carry on living traditions of community gatherings and traditional practices today, we can envision it because as communities today we still gather—to honor loved ones, to acknowledge seasonal changes, to give thanks, to support each other, to keep culture and traditions alive. This takes leadership, hard work, cooperation, respect, and shared values. With World Heritage status we will have not only an opportunity but also a responsibility to engage American Indian Tribal Nations and people today.

The Ohio History Connection is working with Tribal Nations on a regular basis—sharing information about the American Indian sites in its network and finding opportunities to work together. Understanding what is important to Tribal communities and exploring connections between Tribal cultural traditions and the art, iconography, and construction of the earthworks should continue. World Heritage status will create a global stage; the world is the audience, and the curtain is about to rise. Let's rise to the occasion.

The Newark Earthworks Have Integrity

BRAD LEPPER

In order to become a World Heritage Site, you must be able to show that the site has integrity. According to the Operational Guidelines of the World Heritage Convention, integrity means "a measure of the wholeness and intactness" of the site.

Although much of the original Newark Earthworks vanished beneath the plow and the growing City of Newark, local citizens managed to preserve the Great Circle and the Octagon Earthworks. Both sites did suffer some damage, but they are remarkably intact.

The Great Circle became the Licking County Fairgrounds, but the earthworks was one of the main attractions, so any damage to the earthen walls was localized and minimal. In the 1930s, when the site was turned over to the Ohio History Connection, the Civilian Conservation Corps carefully restored the damage.

The Octagon Earthworks includes the large circular enclosure known as the Observatory Circle that is connected to an octagon by a short section of parallel walls. The northern portions of both earthworks were plowed during the 1800s, but the archaeologist Cyrus Thomas, after a careful survey of the site, reported in 1894 that the southern walls of the octagon had never been plowed and remained "almost uninjured, being still more or less covered by the original forest growth." The northernmost walls, which had been plowed for a number of years, nevertheless remained "quite distinct, the height not being less at any point than 2 ½ feet." The original height of the earthwork's walls was nearly six feet.

As for the Observatory Circle, Thomas wrote that its southern half was "yet in the original forest and [had] never been injured by the plow." The northern half, despite having been plowed over, was "yet very distinct, being about 3 feet high at the lowest point."

In 1892, the Octagon Earthworks became the Encampment Ground for the State Militia. James Howe, Adjutant General of the State of Ohio, oversaw the restoration of the damaged portions of the walls. In his 1893 report to the Governor, he stated that "the work at the start was very cautiously proceeded with, and all information which would assist in restoring the grounds to their early condition was eagerly sought for."

So, in 1910, when Moundbuilders County Club took over the site, more than half of the Octagon Earthworks were virtually pristine and the other half had been carefully restored on its substantially intact original foundation.

All of this means that the Great Circle and Octagon Earthworks have high integrity. The earthen walls are mostly whole and intact, including the walls that have been restored. They certainly qualify as a site with "a measure of the wholeness and intactness."

FIGURE 3.2. View of the racetrack that used to run along the upper edge of the Great Circle's moat. Part of the Great Circle's complicated preservation history was as the Licking County Fairgrounds during the second half of the 1800s into the 1930s. Used with permission from the Ohio History Connection.

Designating the Octagon and Great Circle as World Heritage Sites

JENNIFER AULTMAN

I vividly remember the day. I was about ten years old when my family visited Mound City, the 2,000-year-old Hopewell culture earthwork and mound site near Chillicothe, Ohio. Looking across the peaceful, grassy mounds, for the first time in my life I considered that not everyone buries their loved ones in linear cemeteries with engraved stone markers. How were these ancient people different from me, and how were they the same? Standing there with my parents and grandparents, a sharp thought pierced my childhood bubble: the adults who were ever-present in my life would someday be my departed ancestors. It would be my job to see them into the earth, just as the ancient ones did for their ancestors. How would I want my loved ones buried, honored, remembered?

Standing in the real places of history changes us. Today, it is my privilege to coordinate Ohio's effort to add Mound City and seven other sites—including Newark's Octagon and Great Circle Earthworks—to the World Heritage List. A deeply knowledgeable and dedicated team of people from Licking County and across the state has shepherded this work for over a decade. Why? Because we have each had a Mound City moment. We have stood in a place where history was so close, so clear, that it cut through to us in the present and reshaped us. When eight Ohio sites are added to the World Heritage List, all of humanity—present and future—will know to come visit and be changed by the past.

I know that World Heritage Sites have this power because I have worked at one before: Thomas Jefferson's Monticello in Charlottesville, Virginia. Every day, people come from around the world to experience the breathtaking plantation that both sprung from the mind of the author of the Declaration of Independence and was extracted from the toil of people he enslaved against their will. In that complicated place, visitors learn, see, and are transformed. World Heritage Sites let us explore the past to help us figure out how to live in the present.

Perhaps surprisingly, this Virginia past is relevant to Licking County. Thomas Jefferson was fascinated by the ancient Indigenous mounds in Virginia, and he was keenly interested in Ohio's mounds and earthworks. In fact, he knew about the Newark Earthworks. On October 14, 1820, he acknowledged receipt of an early copy of Caleb Atwater's *Description of the Antiquities Discovered in the State of Ohio and Other Western States,* which includes a map and description of the "Ancient Works near Newark, Ohio." I have no doubt that if a World Heritage List had existed in his time, Jefferson would have proposed the Newark Earthworks to join it.

In the end, this intertwined history of earthworks, Jefferson, and me begs the question: why did Thomas Jefferson know about the Newark Earthworks but I, growing up just down the road in Westerville, did not? Remember, my transformational childhood moment happened at Mound City, nearly an hour more distant from my home than Newark. I never heard of the Newark Earthworks back then, and I think it is a travesty that I first learned about them as a student at the University of Virginia, founded by Jefferson.

In the years since, I have had the chance to witness how others find awe at these sacred grounds. I want more Ohioans—and the world—to do the same. World Heritage status will ensure that the Newark Earthworks and the amazing Native history they represent gain the appreciation they deserve.

The Newark Earthworks Have Outstanding Universal Value

BRAD LEPPER

The Newark Earthworks are a monumental masterpiece of Indigenous American religious architecture. Built 2,000 years ago by the Hopewell culture, they are a National Historic Landmark and Ohio's official prehistoric monument. Now they have been nominated to the UNESCO World Heritage List, meaning their significance for all of humanity could soon be recognized globally.

In order to be added to this list of the world's wonders, a site must show that it has "outstanding universal value." That means it must have cultural significance that is "so exceptional as to transcend national boundaries and to be of common importance for present and future generations of all humanity."

That's a high bar, but the Newark Earthworks, as well as the other sites that make up the Hopewell Ceremonial Earthworks nomination, are as amazing as any of the sites already on the World Heritage List. We tend to think of the many separate parts of a site that covers four square miles and that originally included two giant earthen circles, an octagon, a square, and an ellipse, all connected by parallel walled avenues, as separate sites, but they were more like interconnected components of one vast ceremonial earthwork. Thanks to the efforts of the early citizens of Licking County, two of the most important parts of the earthworks survive: the Great Circle and the Octagon Earthworks.

Each earthwork is different, which suggests that each was built for a separate and specialized purpose. The Great Circle, for example, is the only earthwork at Newark with an interior ditch that originally was filled with water. Some early residents mistakenly assumed this meant it was an ancient fort with a moat, but since the moat is on the inside of the walls, we can be fairly certain the Great Circle wasn't a fort.

The giant circular enclosure at the Octagon Earthworks has its own unique feature: a large, flat-topped mound along its southwestern edge. If you stand on that platform and look across the circle along the parallel-walled avenue leading into the octagonal earthworks, you are looking at the point on the horizon where the moon rises at its maximum northern point. That alignment occurs only once every 18.6 years. By aligning the earthworks with the moon's clockwork dance up and down the horizon, these ancient people were linking their most sacred ceremonies with the rhythms of the cosmos.

The Newark Earthworks are every bit as remarkable as the Roman Colosseum or the Great Wall of China, but there's something even more amazing about our earthworks. The Hopewell culture had no kings or emperors to order and manage the construction of monumental architecture. They seemed to have worked cooperatively rather than by coercion. Nor did they live in cities, so there was no guaranteed local labor pool to help build the earthworks. Instead, a Hopewell culture settlement typically consisted of one or a few families living in dispersed settlements with a nearby garden. Everyone lived in the same kinds of houses, ate the same foods, and worked as hard as anyone else. This makes the Hopewell culture special.

These ancient people designed and built enduring monuments on a vast scale, incorporating a deep knowledge of soil engineering, geometry, and astronomy. People from many small communities gathered at these ceremonial centers to cooperate in building the earthworks and to participate in the religious observances that took place there. How they did it is still something of a mystery, but it may be a unique achievement in human history.

How's that for outstanding universal value?

FIGURE 3.3. (*facing*) View of Observatory Mound breaking the otherwise level artificial horizon created by the Octagon's attached Observatory Circle. Photo by John E. Hancock.

46

It Is Time to Prepare for Earthworks Tourism

M. ELIZABETH WEISER

"Ohio was the cultural epicenter of North America two thousand years ago!" announces the Ancient Ohio Trail website.

In my research I travel the world studying how communities represent themselves. I believe we in Ohio have a hard time appreciating the Newark Earthworks in part because it's hard for us to imagine Ohio—or Nerk (as we call our town)—as anything special.

I call this attitude Ohio-humble, and I think it holds us back from seeing the marvel—the world-drawing marvel—that is in our midst. Newark has the largest geometric earthwork complex anywhere on the planet. Anywhere. On the planet. But when I've asked students at The Ohio State University at Newark to name reasons why visitors would come to Licking County, they're often stumped. Easton Mall? The Blue Jackets? Other places have malls and hockey teams (and they're not in our county). The Buckeyes! Okay, I'll grant that one—although believe it or not, other states have college football teams. "Why would anyone come to Ohio?" someone invariably asks.

I moved to Newark from Texas, where everyone had an outsized sense that they were the center of the universe. Ohio is the anti-Texas. "How can I write about my accomplishments without bragging?" students here ask me, and I tell them that as Ohioans, it is genetically impossible for them to brag.

This humbleness can be charming. But not bragging as a community keeps us thinking that our Earthworks simply cannot be that special. We hear the evidence—architecture, geometry, astronomy, artifacts that indicate visitors came from thousands of miles away—but still we wonder. We argue over whether a site unique in the world has enough "outstanding universal value" to qualify for World Heritage status even after the world tells us that it does.

Instead, we should spend time preparing. Tourism companies, guidebooks, websites, travel magazines all give prominence to World Heritage Sites. An Ohio University study estimates a 100% increase in visitors within three years of inscription. Are we ready?

The World Heritage Site of Cahokia, "America's first city," consisting of a mound complex built 1,200 years later than our Earthworks, sits across the river from St. Louis and next door to Collinsville, Illinois. The state of Illinois built a visitor center at Cahokia which drew 500,000 visitors a year for decades.

According to scholars of World Heritage Sites, increased economic benefit to a community depends greatly on how the community responds, how business and tourism sectors work together with caretakers, how the site is promoted and interpreted, and what amenities are provided. With the Earthworks, we can connect the innovative visions that produced Newark the city in the nineteenth and twentieth centuries with the innovative visions that produced the Octagon and Great Circle 2,000 years earlier. We can expand the already growing linkages between local businesses, academic and cultural institutions to reframe the story of Ohio pre- and post-contact and make our town a destination.

We can be the place where visitors from around the world come to see a remarkable site interpreted for them through a comprehensive visitor center, perhaps add in a visit to local museums and then spend a night in one of our pleasant hotels, eat at a local restaurant, maybe catch some music downtown, buy souvenirs as they wander our shops, and enjoy the outdoors in our parks and rivers.

When they leave, I want them to remember that they were at the NEWARK Earthworks—but for that to happen, we in Ohio have to believe it first.

What Can America Learn from the Hopewell Ceremonial Earthworks?

RICHARD D. SHIELS

What will our earthworks teach the world once they become a World Heritage Site?

Try this answer: Long before Europeans arrived, about the time of Julius Caesar and Jesus Christ, Ohio was home to a brilliant Indigenous culture. And then let me suggest something even bigger.

The Newark Earthworks are Indigenous mounds of a certain type: earthen enclosures—spaces you can walk into, defined by earthen walls. They once included four huge geometric enclosures, connected by passageways defined by earthen walls that may very well have been connected to similar structures seventy miles away in Chillicothe, Ohio.

These four enclosures demonstrate a sophisticated knowledge of geometry and an astounding knowledge of astronomy. Ohio State University history professor Lucy Murphy calls our earthworks "Native knowledge written on the land."

Ancestors of today's Native people built an amazing number of earthen enclosures over a 500-year period beginning about 100 BCE. One map shows the location of 586 earthen enclosures within the boundaries of today's Ohio. The vast majority were geometric: circles, squares, combinations of circles and squares, and, in two places, an octagon connected to a circle. A much smaller number, called hilltop forts, followed the curvature of the top of a hill. Hundreds of earthen enclosures built over 400 years across the southern half of Ohio constitute clear evidence of a long-standing brilliant Native culture.

Chillicothe, which is today home to Hopewell Culture National Historical Park, was the hub of this ancient culture. Chillicothe featured multiple impressive enclosures, including the only other octagon-connected-to-a-circle ever built. Former park ranger Bruce Lombardo liked to say, "If Julius Caesar had sent a delegation to North America, they would have gone to Chillicothe." The most impressive hilltop fort is still standing outside of Lebanon, Ohio. Archaeologists named it Fort Ancient although none of these enclosures were, in fact, forts. The Hopewell Ceremonial Earthworks nomination that includes Hopewell Culture National Historical Park, Fort Ancient, and Newark tells the story of a brilliant culture here in Ohio 2,000 years ago. Together with other World Heritage Sites, they tell an even bigger story.

Two of the current twenty-four World Heritage Sites in the United States focus on Indigenous earthworks in eastern North America. These are Poverty Point in Louisiana and Cahokia in Illinois. The earthworks at Poverty Point were built 3500 years ago. Cahokia was a city of 20,000–30,000 people (and fifty-five remarkable mounds) less than 800 years ago. Our 2,000-year-old earthworks are the center of that story. Together these three sites teach us that brilliant cultures came and went over thousands of years prior to the supposed "discovery" of the "New World."

American history did not begin in 1492, and today's textbooks do not begin with Christopher Columbus. Often, they begin with Cahokia. I like to say Cahokia has cracked the textbooks. I have twice taken groups to Cahokia and asked the site manager how that happened. Here is his answer: "We became a World Heritage Site."

World Heritage will change the story we call American history.

FIGURE 4.1. Visitors to the Great Circle taking in the site. Photo by John E. Hancock.

PART IV

Experiencing and Remembering Earthworks

The Newark Earthworks are the most intact geometric earthworks anywhere. Nowhere else can visitors walk between the walls of this type of earthwork and know they are surrounded by much of the original 2,000-year-old structure. Wandering the grounds can be a powerful experience in simply being, but these sites also can spur contemplation of the things that people once did within them. Alongside the distinct shapes of the Great Circle and Octagon also stand walkway remnants that point to the portions of the larger complex that are no longer visible, adding to the questions about the possibilities for these sites.

Places of Spirituality, Accomplishment, and Power

MARTI L. CHAATSMITH

Over the past fifteen years, I have been privileged to host guests of the Newark Earthworks Center—teachers, artists, researchers, journalists, American Indian leaders—as they walked through the earthworks for the first time. As our guests moved along the grassy embankments to enter the elegant enclosures, I witnessed wonder and awe as they listened to our descriptions of the Hopewell Ceremonial Earthworks, in particular the only two remaining original earthworks: the beautiful and enigmatic Octagon Earthworks and the fascinating Great Circle.

These earthworks are places of accomplishment, spirituality, and power, conveying a worldview we don't fully comprehend. They are spiritual places, revealing what we share with the people of the Hopewell culture: the urgency of bringing life into this world, embracing the challenges of living and loving with purpose, and the separation of those we love from this world in recognition of the finality of death. The ancient people believed that everything in their world contained sparks of life—water and air, animals and plants, different kinds of earth and rocks, under the sky and stars. By taking this living material and shaping it precisely into gigantic shapes aligned to the recurring events around them, the people were gathering life force to create places of power.

"What do American Indian people think of the earthworks?" This is a frequently asked question as I lead tours of the Octagon and Great Circle. I am American Indian—a citizen of the Comanche Nation of Oklahoma from my mother's family and a direct descendant of the Choctaw Nation of Oklahoma from my father's family. While being Native does not necessarily provide answers, it does provide an essential framework with which to see the earthworks from Indigenous perspectives.

When I arrived to work at the Newark Earthworks Center in 2004, I could only see golfing at the Octagon. For a long time, I kept returning, standing on the observation platform overlooking the walled path that links the octagon to the circle or walking along the sidewalk while hawks glided overhead. During the Open House days, when the entire site opens to visitors, I spent time down at the creek where people might have disembarked from canoes, watching herons wading in the water. Gradually, my personal understanding of the Octagon began to take shape; something about being in a space where so many of the original people of this continent gathered in the light of the moon every nineteen years at a place engineered to focus our attention on the intersection of land and sky, humans and the natural world.

Many of our Native guests respond to their experiences at the earthworks by seeking a personal connection to being at an ancestral site. They veer off from the formal tours to walk beside the long walls, sit quietly at the entrance of the Great Circle or stand in the middle of the Octagon. Native heritage stretches back thousands of years and forward to the present day. Tribal nations continue to share their histories and knowledge of living in the Ohio Valley woodlands and inform our understanding of ancient, sacred places. The stories we learn about Ohio's earthworks begin with the brilliant people who built them and will be continued by honoring their accomplishments with respect and love.

The First Modern Lunar Standstill

MIKE MICKELSON

What was it like for the Indigenous constructors of the earthworks to see the moonrise 2,000 years ago? Evidence of lunar standstills is encoded into the architecture of various archaeological sites worldwide, and awareness of this cyclic lunar event must have been a part of the fabric of knowledge of the builders of the Newark Earthworks and their ancestors. It might be presumed that as the Octagon and its related earthworks were laid out, many such moonrises were observed. In use, was this event a moment of celebration or religious adoration of the moon as it entered the Octagon? Was it a place of worship, or a sophisticated lunar calendar? These are enduring questions.

What we do know is that early in this century we in Newark marked the first modern observation of the lunar standstill. As we approached the time when the rising moon moved to its farthest point to the north along the eastern horizon, a few of us were keen to view, and, for me, to test the calculations of Ray Hively and Bob Horn.

As the 2006 major lunar standstill period approached, we knew we should see the moon rise in alignment along the primary axis of the Octagon. Since this extreme standstill only slowly changes over a period of a couple of years (that is why it is called a standstill), every month the moon would rise at very nearly the same northern location on the horizon. In October of 2005, we calculated the time of the maximum northern moonrise and headed to the Octagon Circle's Observatory Mound to make our observation. The moon rose directly along the Octagon's main axis. Hively and Horn's hypothesis was correct! The builders of the Octagon Earthworks had indeed built the lunar standstill into their massive structure. We experienced what they had so many centuries before.

We don't know how many years, or centuries, this event was witnessed by ancient people, but we know we were the first in many, many years—centuries? millennia?—to purposely observe this phenomenon. Brad Lepper, Dick Shiels, Jeff Gill, and I experienced what those ancients saw—for us, a very emotional event. In my case as an astronomer, I confirmed the hypothesis proposed by Hively and Horn. The experience was quite a different one for each of us, as words fail to adequately describe the awe we collectively felt.

FIGURE 4.2. (*facing*) The curve of Observatory Circle from the base of Observatory Mound. Photo by Timothy E. Black.

Complicated History Is Built into Our Landscape

M. ELIZABETH WEISER

On Thanksgiving Day of 2015, we gathered with our Ohio family—our closest friends—to celebrate. We had all moved here from elsewhere; our three girls have grown up together. We had the traditional turkey and sides; we shared our memories of past Thanksgivings together and apart; we stuffed ourselves with pie.

And then we bundled up and went to the Octagon Earthworks, where we walked across the dark grounds and sat together in the still, cool night, waiting for the minimum northern moonrise, halfway through the long cycle, to rise along its designated mound axis. In November in Ohio, it was a gamble that the clouds would clear enough. But we sat together, just being quiet, watching our girls being a little less quiet, as the night drew on.

I found myself thinking about the people who had sat here all those generations ago—the ones who had also known which was the correct night to watch the full moon rise along which exact sightline in the giant earthen complex they had built. Maybe some of them, like us, had traveled to the area from afar. Maybe these important markers in the long calendar were also holidays to them, as this one happened to be for us that night. Maybe there'd also been a special meal somewhere nearby, families and friends gathered around fires, sharing stories and memories. Surely their children were also playing before them, and the adults no doubt reflected on the passing years. I know I thought about how small the three girls had been at the last major marker—the maximum northern moon rising 9.3 years earlier—how they were now beloved teenagers, how inconceivably old they'd all

be at that next maximum rising in far-distant 2025. I wondered where we'd all be in our lives by then. Watching for the moonrise was watching the passage of time. I'm sure it must have felt that way for ancient people as well.

I've traveled the world multiple times. It no longer surprises me to find that we humans have remarkably similar hopes, dreams, desires for our lives and our children. If the past is an undiscovered country, it's a country peopled with recognizable humans. Sitting there that night, I thought about how, like people today, and like the builders of Newark, Ohio, in the nineteenth and twentieth centuries, these were people who imagined something bigger than what *was,* and they set out together to build it. In some complex mix of motivations—religious, social, scientific curiosity, artistic imagination—they noticed, they studied, they organized, they built, they got the word out, they hosted, they tended—and families like ours came to participate and be awed.

But then, at some point, this place stopped being quite so important to them. And then later new people came, refugees from the rising flood of immigrants (like the Pilgrims) who were taking over their Eastern Seaboard. And then the descendants of those immigrants also moved westward, becoming the settlers who founded and built the town they called Newark. Their interactions with the Native people already here were often fraught, and in 1832, the Indian Removal Act forced those original inhabitants out of the state or underground.

And still the town grew. Fields that fed the people also plowed over the earthworks, and railroads linking them to the world also tore up burial sites. Townspeople fought to preserve what was left and then did so by playing golf—but still the earthworks were preserved. Today we might soon be welcoming the world again, just as those ancient builders did, and just as the townsfolk who planned the Ohio-Erie canal and the railroad and the National Road envisioned.

It's a complicated history.

We hear a lot of talk these days about the supposed dangers of teaching and learning a version of American history that acknowledges its many complications. But here in Ohio we have a way to see past the limited, untruthful story that there's only *one* story. In Newark, in the nearly 600 earthworks sites in our state, in the settlements that fall and rise, we can see the many complicated histories built into our very landscape. Many and different people built our story, with many and the same kinds of joys and sorrows, despairs and dreams.

As the moon rose in front of our three girls that Thanksgiving evening, on a sightline built into the earth by people 2,000 years before, I gave my own thanks for the messy, complicated, extraordinary history that was all around them. By the next moonrise in the long cycle, they would be the new generation carrying us forward. It was time to make sure they knew the stories.

Generations of Learners Honor the Earthworks

MARY F. BORGIA

My mother was born here in Newark, Ohio, just a couple of months after the stock market crash of 1929. Sadly, she passed away this summer, and I faced the task of sorting through the treasures of her long and eventful life. My heart melted when I discovered a large tote with a note on top that read, "Mary's Accounts of Earthworks Projects." An entire tote, dedicated to following activities related to the Newark Earthworks. Why would all this mean so much to her?

Let me catch you up. Many years ago, I was lucky enough to be a fourth-grade teacher at William E. Miller Elementary. At that time, there were no walls between the classrooms. Every day my students would venture to the other side of the chalkboard to be taught social studies by the incredible Bill Hughes, who had developed a remarkable curriculum about the prehistory of Ohio. As videos played, I would hear Brad Lepper's voice telling me about the astounding mathematical precision of our Newark Earthworks, and I would be swept away by tales of how a culture known as the Hopewell built earthworks and created artwork made from materials from all over the country.

When Mr. Hughes retired, I jumped at the opportunity to teach social studies. That year, a group of students became so excited about what they were learning that they wanted to do something important to honor the Newark Earthworks. They conducted research and then made several trips to the Ohio State House, where they presented their findings to members of the state legislature. Thanks to their efforts, the Newark Earthworks are designated as the "official prehis-

toric monument of the state of Ohio." The signing was celebrated on a beautiful June day in 2006, where hundreds of students walked solemnly onto the Octagon portion of the Newark Earthworks, accompanied by drumming and singing from members of the Native American Indian Center of Central Ohio. Governor Bob Taft himself came to the dedication ceremony.

And suddenly the Newark Earthworks were everywhere! Soon I was participating in a Fulbright Teacher exchange with a teacher who lived near Stonehenge. For one semester he taught in my classroom in Newark, and I taught his students in Salisbury. Our students discovered remarkable similarities between the Newark Earthworks and Stonehenge. The earthen walls surrounding Stonehenge look so much like our Great Circle! The entry points into the monuments from the surrounding rivers were remarkably similar. I also discovered an elaborate display on the Newark Earthworks at the British Museum in London.

You may wonder how this relates to my opening story about my mother. She lived in this town for almost eighty years before she learned that her "picnic spot" was a stunning collection of earthen geometry that was worthy of a World Heritage designation. She lived somewhere as amazing as Stonehenge! She could scarcely believe the beauty of the Shaman of Newark and other pieces of Native art discovered locally. She was always talking about how much this town would benefit once the Earthworks become a World Heritage Site, and she was so excited about all the work being done to educate others about it. I was not taught about Ohio's earthworks when I was younger, either, but now there is a wealth of information available so that everyone can learn about the magnificence of the Hopewell Ceremonial Earthworks.

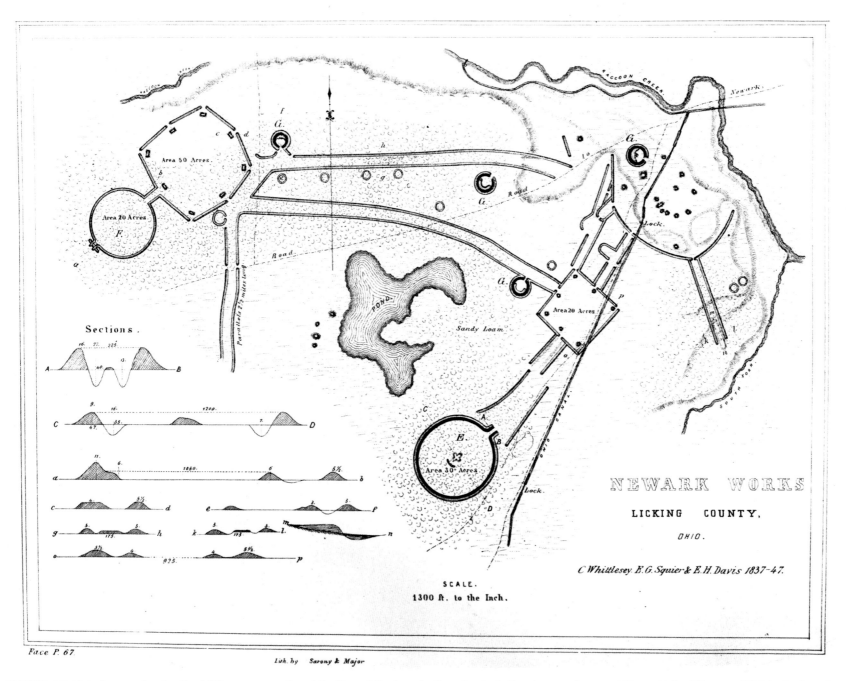

FIGURE 4.3. Historic map showing the full four square miles of the Newark Earthworks Complex, including the now destroyed Cherry Valley Ellipse and Wright Earthworks and the walkways that connected them to the Great Circle and Octagon. This map first appeared in E. G. Squier and E. H. Davis's 1848 book *Ancient Monuments of the Mississippi Valley*. Used with permission from the Ohio History Connection.

The Other Newark Earthworks

TIMOTHY R. W. JORDAN

Visitors to the Great Circle and Octagon are often fascinated to learn that the Newark Earthworks once included two other major shapes: a nearly perfect square and an enormous oval. This square and oval were connected by walled walkways that covered over four square miles. Their interconnectedness is part of why we call the Newark Earthworks a complex.

A remnant of the square still exists. Officially it is called the Wright Earthworks and lies in a green space owned by the Ohio History Connection at the intersection of James and Waldo Streets in Newark. It is about a half-mile to the northeast of the Great Circle, with the two, low, free-standing walls that run on either side of the site's museum pointing off in its direction.

Whatever the significance of the Wright Square, with its long walls averaging 931 feet, surveying maps from the 1800s show that it was the only one of the four major shapes connected to all three of the others by low-walled walkways. In addition to the Great Circle to the southwest, the oval shape was another half-mile to the northeast, and the Octagon was a full mile to the northwest. Apparently, passing through the Wright Square was necessary for going between any two of the other shapes. The remnant of Wright is so small that it's impossible to tell the original orientation of its corners, but John Low (Pokagon Band of Potawatomi), the director of The Ohio State University's Newark Earthworks Center, and I have wondered about the northerly direction in which the corner would seem to have pointed. Thinking about the cardinal directions adds to the sense of movement at that site.

The oval shape, what we call the Cherry Valley Ellipse, was situated to the northeast of the Wright Earthworks, where Union St. and Wehrle Ave. now run. Although a placard commemorating the Ellipse as the complex's burial ground stands on the southeast side of the Union St. railroad crossing, no portion of the huge earthwork—which measured 1800 feet long and encompassed a fifty-acre area—remains visible.

Ignorance and racism certainly contributed to the destruction of the Ellipse and the Wright Square, but a series of nineteenth-century survey maps reveal another factor that's not as easy to dismiss. Chronologically lining up these maps shows the Ohio-Erie Canal as among the first features built by settlers to encroach upon the sites. It cut south from Raccoon Creek through the center of the Ellipse and clipped a corner of Wright. Water was an important resource for both Native and settler cultures. This fact should not excuse the ignorance and racism, but it should sit uncomfortably for us. Even more uncomfortable is the evidence that portions of burial mounds from the Ellipse were incorporated into the nineteenth-century Union St. railroad embankment.

Nevertheless, there are lessons beyond archaeology that still can be learned from these destroyed sites. In 2011, representatives from the Newark Earthworks Center brought to a meeting of the Ohio Rail

Development Commission evidence of burial mounds from the Ellipse being incorporated into the embankment. As a result, it was written into the lease for that stretch of track that whenever maintenance is done an archaeologist must be present, based on the possibility that funerary materials and cultural artifacts are embedded within the embankment.

So, what's the lesson? We can't change the past but understanding it can shape the decisions we make now and for the future. That's why it's important to remember the Wright Square and the Ellipse. It's also another reason why the Great Circle and Octagon, with Fort Ancient and Hopewell Culture National Historical Park, deserve World Heritage recognition.

The Life-Changing Potential of Our Earthworks

RICHARD D. SHIELS

Learning about the brilliance of ancient Ohioans who built the earthworks can change our understanding of history—and for some it can change their life. Let me give you one example.

About three years ago, I met a Native American man when we were participating in a walk that Jeff Gill led through the city of Newark. Jeff points out fragments of the 2,000-year-old Newark Earthworks that remain throughout the city, outside of the Great Circle and the Octagon. The hike takes all morning, and there is ample time to talk along the way.

On that day I met a Dakota man and his two adult sons. He spoke about growing up on a reservation in North Dakota. Tragically, he said, he grew up believing that Indians are descended from savages. He internalized the notion that Indians are stupid because that is what he was told in school and by the culture as a whole. Consequently, he had believed that he was much less intelligent than people of other races. He spoke particularly about a meeting in the weeks approaching high school graduation in which his Caucasian teachers had advised him not to expect a career. For years he lived with this false sense of inferiority.

Then he began telling me about our Earthworks. He had attended our first Newark Earthworks Day on the Ohio State Newark campus in 2005 and remembered much of what he'd learned. He spoke with great enthusiasm, and his recollection of the information was entirely accurate. He explained the geometry of the Great Circle and the astronomy of the lunar alignments at the Octagon. He made me marvel anew at the brilliance of the ancient people. With a big smile he concluded that "we were not savages." We Indians were not savages.

Learning about the Earthworks "changed my life," he said. A new sense of American Indian accomplishment enabled him to change his diet and his demeanor. "It changed the way I raised my sons," he said with a smile. I am smiling as I write this: it changed his life!

The stories we tell our children and ourselves have an impact. The historical images we teach in our schools and internalize in our minds determine our sense of ourselves. Americans of European descent benefit from the history our schools teach them. It is time we extend that benefit to all children. We need to teach more than the cultures that arose in Europe. It is time we teach all our children about the brilliant Indigenous cultures that rose and fell and survived over the millennia here in America—indeed, right here in Ohio!

FIGURE 4.4. (*following*) Visitors to the Great Circle walking in the site's monumental gateway. Photo by John E. Hancock.

Thin Places

JIM WILLIAMS

Heaven and earth, according to Celtic spirituality, are only three feet apart, but in thin places that distance is even shorter. A thin place can be a place where we can catch a glimpse of the infinite in the midst of the ordinary.

Coming out of Indigenous traditions, the Newark Earthworks is just such a place. Maybe my Welsh/Celtic roots are showing, but I am drawn to places like this. Here is a place where I can breathe again.

Recently I had a conversation with another site interpreter who has had a great deal of experience leading tours in the Earthworks. He told me about a time when he was just beginning to lead tours and lost his bearings inside both the Great Circle and the Octagon. It happens more easily than one might think.

Entering these massive geometric earthworks, one loses a sense of the horizon beyond the mounded earth walls. There is earth and there is sky. I can imagine how it might have been for those who constructed the Newark Earthworks and gathered there. Ordinary time and orientation slip away.

Some people describe similar experiences when visiting Gothic cathedrals with their soaring ceilings, or when gazing out on a lake or ocean when the sky is perfectly dark.

Walking the grounds of the Great Circle or the Octagon does not necessarily lead to anything as grandiose as a spiritual awakening, but it can disorient and confuse. You can lose your bearings and have to find a new way, as it challenges you to reorient and rethink your tired old ways of seeing the world.

One interpretation of the Newark Earthworks is that a Native person 2,000 or more years ago had a spiritual vision, and that vision inspired a generation of people to invest their time and talents to construct this marvel. Imagine how that vision inspired folks to develop a plan that went into how they were going to feed, house, and bathe all the gathered people during the construction. Imagine the vision and charisma of the leaders of this project to get all the people involved, select gifted astronomers, mathematicians, and engineers, and then orchestrate the direction and building of this place without the benefit of email, snail mail, or microphones.

People from all over the world have come to visit the Newark Earthworks. Some come to check it off their list of World Heritage Site candidates. Some come because of their notion that the site conceals a hidden meaning. Some come because it is a good place to walk the dog on a pleasant day.

Sometimes the space feels very ordinary. A picnic table is just a picnic table for a short lunch hour on a busy day. That's okay. Ordinary earth and sky, grass and air, food and water, and people gathered are how the sacred gets in.

To all the visitors that come, I remind them that behind all the facts and the wonder, here lies a special place. One that has been a sacred place—a thin place—for over 2,000 years.

Thinking about Earthworks in New Ways

TIMOTHY R. W. JORDAN

Like many Licking Countians, I must make a confession: I used to walk along the top of the Great Circle's wall.

It's a practice we now discourage. More and more in the last twenty years we have realized how a healthy layer of grass forms such a tight seal that it is the best protection against erosion for an earthwork. Nevertheless, my memories of time spent at the site with loved ones remain fond ones—of grandparents who've now been gone for more than a decade; of a sister who now lives out of state; of a brother whose work puts him in circles very different from my own for weeks at a time.

For all that, walking along the interior of the Great Circle's wall instead of its top offers an even more powerful experience. The curve of the earthwork and its moat suggests a very logical path to follow. The distance of nearly three-quarters of a mile along flat ground with a consistent arc easily allows a visitor to establish a steady cadence while walking.

The site directs attention as well as movement. To one side the wall is bordered above and below by moat and sky. Such three-part layering—water, earth, sky—may reflect Indigenous cosmological beliefs on the division of the universe. It's an idea posed by the archaeologists and historians who've worked with the Ancient Ohio Trail website. It also mirrors ideas presented in such stories as David Cusick's telling of the Haudenosaunee Creation story and Edward Benton-Banai's *Mishomis Book,* an Ojibwe collection.

Sounds are also different while walking through the Great Circle. The earthen wall noticeably dampens the noises from outside of it. The effect helps to focus attention on what's most immediate to that place and time. Birdsong. Footsteps. Rustling leaves and grass. Breathing.

In all these ways, the Great Circle creates a sense of order and balance. Walking through it can be powerfully meditative, either alone or with others.

During my time as an interpreter at the Newark Earthworks, I have had the privilege to work and develop friendships with several Native people. Although these friends are quick to say they do not speak for all Indigenous people, I always appreciate how their observations have deepened my experience of what it means to be at an earthworks site.

The language we use to describe the sites is one such way. Marti Chaatsmith (Comanche, Choctaw), associate director of the Earthworks Center at OSU Newark, once shared with me a tribal representative's use of the phrase *Earthen Circle* instead of *Great Circle*. The shift moves us from thinking sheerly about size to something much more nurturing.

In a similar vein, the Earthworks Center Director John Low (Pokagon Band of Potawatomi) has commented on how the words *dirt* and *soil* can imply uncleanliness, but the associations of *Mother Earth* are supremely sacred.

World Heritage will continue to alter the way those of us who have long lived near the earthworks at Newark, Chillicothe, and Lebanon think about these sites, but as we move beyond personal memories to experiencing earthworks in new ways, how amazing can those changes in our understandings be!

FIGURE 5.1. (*following*) Aerial photo showing how, as a hilltop enclosure, the walls of Fort Ancient accent the natural contours of the raised land upon which the site is built. Photo by Timothy E. Black.

PART V

The Ohio Phenomenon

The Hopewell Ceremonial Earthworks World Heritage nomination encompasses more than Newark's Great Circle and Octagon. Also included in this nomination are the Fort Ancient Earthworks and five of the earthworks managed by the National Parks Service as Hopewell Culture National Historical Park. Fort Ancient is another Ohio History Connection site that serves as the premiere example of a hilltop enclosure. Hopewell Culture National Historical Park provides the most complete artifact record of any set of Hopewell sites. As a serial nomination, these eight earthworks provide multiple access points to the ancient Hopewell culture through three modern Ohio counties: Licking, Warren, and Ross.

World Heritage for the Hopewell Culture Earthworks

RICHARD D. SHIELS

Newark's Octagon and Great Circle Earthworks have recently been nominated for the UNESCO World Heritage List by the United States Department of Interior. World Heritage is a UNESCO program intended to preserve the most important historical and cultural sites across the globe. There are over 1,100 such officially recognized sites. Receiving World Heritage status often results in a significant increase in visitation and public awareness.

World Heritage was an American idea, proposed by Lydon B. Johnson's White House in 1965 and implemented in 1972 during Richard Nixon's presidency. It was fashioned after the National Park Service. There are currently twenty-four World Heritage Sites in the United States, including the Grand Canyon, Yellowstone, Mesa Verde, Independence Hall, and two mound sites: Cahokia in Illinois and Poverty Point in Louisiana.

Our World Heritage nomination, entitled "Hopewell Ceremonial Earthworks," includes earthworks in three separate Ohio counties. The Ohio History Connection (OHC) owns the Newark Earthworks and Fort Ancient in Warren County; the National Park System owns the five sites at Hopewell Culture National Historical Park in Chillicothe. World Heritage will not change the ownership or control of these sites. Together they tell a great big story about a brilliant ancient culture we call Hopewell.

Central Ohio people have been advocating for World Heritage status for the Newark Earthworks for nearly twenty years. In 2002–2003 a committee of nearly forty of us (including the leadership of the Moundbuilders Country Club) was appointed by the OHC (then called the Ohio Historical Society, OHS) to write a long-term plan. In it we called upon OHS to pursue World Heritage at the next opportunity. A year or two later the superintendent of Hopewell Culture National Historical Park (HCNHP) in Chillicothe suggested that we work together to achieve World Heritage designation for earthworks at both our sites.

When in 2009 the Department of the Interior put out a call for sites within the United States that might be considered for nomination, OHS and HCNHP submitted a proposal jointly. Fifty-five proposals were considered from across the nation. The Interior Department submitted a list of ten of them to UNESCO the next year. Several of these have become World Heritage Sites since that time. We are next on the list. National Park Service Director Chuck Sams said that "the Hopewell Ceremonial Earthworks are an important example of the ancient history of the Indigenous peoples of America that help us tell the world the whole story of America and the remarkable diversity of our cultural heritage." We are hopeful that all involved will see the benefits of designating these Ohio masterworks as World Heritage Sites.

UNESCO requires that any nomination must demonstrate that the site in question meets one of ten criteria. Dr. Bradley Lepper argues that our earthworks meet all ten. However, on the advice of the Department of Interior, our nomination materials focus upon two criteria that everyone agrees we clearly meet:

- to bear a unique or at least exceptional testimony to a cultural tradition or to a civilization which is living or which has disappeared; and
- to represent a masterpiece of human creative genius.

Great things are on the horizon for the Hopewell Ceremonial Earthworks.

The Fort Ancient Earthworks: Similar but Different

BRAD LEPPER

The Fort Ancient Earthworks in Warren County is the largest and best preserved of the Hopewell hilltop enclosures, and it is a part of the nomination to the UNESCO World Heritage List as the Hopewell Ceremonial Earthworks. As a hilltop enclosure, it shares important similarities with geometric earthworks such as the Newark Earthworks, but there are important differences as well.

Fort Ancient consists of 3.5 miles of earthen walls that vary in height from three to twenty-three feet. These walls enclose the top of a large bluff that overlooks the Little Miami River. The earthworks has two main parts, the so-called North and South Forts, and a narrow set of walls connecting the two, known as the Middle Fort.

Despite its name, Fort Ancient was not a fort. Ditches that held water run alongside most walls, but they are located mostly inside the walls rather than outside, where a defensive moat would have been placed. In addition, there are more than sixty openings or gateways in the walls, which would have made the "fort" difficult to defend.

Fort Ancient now is understood to have been mainly a place of ceremony, though since there are very few burial mounds at the site, mortuary ceremonies don't seem to have been as important here as they were at many of the geometric earthworks.

Four small stone-covered mounds in the North Fort, which did not contain burials, are arranged in a perfect square 512 feet on a side. Standing at the westernmost mound, you can view the summer solstice sunrise as well as the maximum and minimum moonrises through three consecutive gateways in the eastern enclosure wall. Fort Ancient, therefore, like Newark's Octagon Earthworks, was linked to the rhythms of the cosmos.

Recent research has revealed the remains of a woodhenge in the North Fort that consisted of three concentric rings of large posts. The outermost circle was about 200 feet in diameter. At the center of the circle, there was a central basin in which the people had built a low mound of red clay—perhaps as an altar. After the last ceremony was performed here, they decommissioned the site by removing the wooden posts and burying it beneath layers of gravel hauled up from the bed of the Little Miami River. Dr. Robert Riordan, the archaeologist who has been studying the site for the last sixteen years, named it the Moorehead Circle to honor the early archaeologist who worked at Fort Ancient and who is largely responsible for preserving the site. Riordan thinks the Moorehead Circle was the ceremonial heart of Fort Ancient.

Six hundred or so years later, a different group of Native people established a large village and cemetery in the South Fort. Early archaeologists incorrectly assumed these villagers were the builders of Fort Ancient. Following the convention of naming newly identified cultures after the places they were first recognized, they called it the Fort Ancient culture. So, not only is the Fort Ancient Earthworks not a fort, but the Fort Ancient culture didn't build it.

By combining Fort Ancient with Newark's Great Circle and Octagon Earthworks and the earthworks of Hopewell Culture National Historical Park into a single World Heritage nomination, we can tell a more complete story about this amazing culture and gain a fuller appreciation for the scope and grandeur of their architectural achievements.

FIGURE 5.2. Mound City, one of the Hopewell Culture National Historical Park's sites, features burial mounds, an exterior wall, and reflecting pools. Photo by John E. Hancock.

Hopewell Culture National Historical Park: The Hopewell Core

BRET J. RUBY

The five earthworks included in Hopewell Culture National Historical Park (NHP) in Ross County, near Chillicothe, make some special contributions to the overall nomination of the Hopewell Ceremonial Earthworks. The earthworks found here have a long history of study that continues to this day, and much of what we know about the Hopewell period was learned in this area. They have been a focus for tourism, recreation, research, and education for more than 100 years, and World Heritage listing will increase these opportunities.

Archaeologists recognize the region surrounding the confluence of the Scioto River and Paint Creek in Ross County as the Hopewell core. Nowhere else in the world can one find such a spectacular concentration of geometric earthworks. More than two dozen of the largest earthwork enclosures are found within thirty miles of Chillicothe, along with most of the largest Hopewell mounds.

Some of the earliest scientific attempts to understand who built these earthworks and why were made at these Ross County sites. Two Chillicothe residents—Ephraim Squier and Edwin Davis—carefully measured and mapped the most impressive earthworks surrounding their homes in the 1840s. They excavated dozens of mounds. Their efforts to carefully record and publish their findings set them apart from unscientific relic hunters.

Some of Squier and Davis's most important discoveries were made at the Mound City Group earthworks, now the centerpiece of Hopewell Culture NHP. Here they found tobacco smoking pipes masterfully carved into realistic images of birds, mammals, and amphib-

ians. Tobacco continues to be smoked as a sacrament in Indigenous religious ceremonies today.

The Mound City pipes were burned and broken before being deposited on carefully prepared clay altars. These were among the first clues that what we call *Hopewell* is not one people, but a set of religious beliefs and practices expressed in sacred objects and earthworks: an Indigenous religious movement that spread across many distinct cultures and half the continent nearly 2,000 years ago. Many of the beautiful and finely crafted sacred objects made and used at the earthworks were fashioned from exotic raw materials obtained from distant parts of North America, including copper from the Great Lakes, marine shell from the Gulf of Mexico, and obsidian from Yellowstone National Park. Most of these artistic masterpieces were originally deposited at the earthworks sites now included in Hopewell Culture NHP. Research to understand and appreciate the minds and motivations of these Indigenous peoples continues today.

These early discoveries led directly to the establishment of Mound City Group National Monument in 1923. In 1992, the park was expanded with the addition of Hopeton Earthworks, High Bank Works, Seip Earthworks, and the Hopewell Mound Group, and renamed as Hopewell Culture National Historical Park. Designation as a World Heritage Site will expand our ability to meet our original and ongoing mission to preserve, protect, and educate the world about the human creative genius embodied in this Indigenous heritage.

How the Great Hopewell Road Connected Newark with Chillicothe

BRAD LEPPER

The Newark Earthworks are one of the most magnificent of the Hopewell ceremonial centers, but they are seemingly isolated from the Hopewell heartland. Newark is located sixty miles to the north of the largest concentration of earthworks along the Scioto River Valley and its tributaries near modern Chillicothe. There is, however, compelling evidence to suggest that, far from being isolated, they are linked directly to that heart of the Hopewell world by a major transportation artery.

The Great Hopewell Road is a set of low earthen walls framing a 200-foot-wide avenue that extended from the southernmost gateway of Newark's Octagon Earthworks for an undetermined distance to the southwest. In the 1860s, James and Charles Salisbury traced the walls "some 6 miles over fertile fields, through tangled swamps and across streams, still keeping their undeviating course." They didn't follow the road to its destination but suggested that, if it continued in its perfectly straight course, it would lead to Chillicothe.

If we eventually find that the Great Hopewell Road actually did go all the way to Chillicothe, it won't be all that surprising. We've known for a long time that there was a special relationship between these special places.

High Bank Works, part of Hopewell Culture National Historical Park, and Newark's Octagon Earthworks are the only large circles connected to octagons built by the Hopewell culture. The circles at both sites are the same size and both earthworks are aligned to the key points on the horizon that circumscribe the Moon's complicated 18.6-year-long cycle of shifting risings and settings.

But why would the Hopewell have needed an avenue to connect them equivalent in size to a modern sixteen-lane freeway? (The busiest freeway in Los Angeles is only fourteen lanes.) Why did it need to be so straight?

I think the Great Hopewell Road was a sacred processional path used by pilgrims to travel to Newark's gigantic earthen cathedral. The Maya civilization had similar long, straight roads. When Spanish priests asked the Maya about their purpose, the people told them the roads were routes of pilgrimage that connected their most sacred places.

The Creek Indians of the southeastern United States have a tradition that they once traveled to the north on periodic pilgrimages to "special mounds" that were important for "ritual interactions with the cosmos." We don't know whether those special mounds were as far north as Newark, but the Octagon Earthworks, with its precise alignments to the rising and setting of the moon, certainly could have facilitated ritual interactions with the cosmos.

Pilgrims may have come to Newark bearing offerings of thanksgiving or supplication from their homelands. This may explain the artifacts found in Hopewell mounds made of copper from the Great Lakes, shells from the Gulf of Mexico, and mica from the southern Appalachian Mountains. Archaeologists have found small blades made from our local Flint Ridge flint at Hopewell-era sites across eastern North

America. These may have been tokens given to pilgrims in acknowledgment of their spiritual and literal journeys.

The idea that the Newark Earthworks were a pilgrimage center may explain why the site is so enormous. It was not built to serve only a local congregation; it was built to share with the world. And the Great Hopewell Road was built to a similar scale—not necessarily to accommodate thousands of processioners at once, but certainly to impress pilgrims with the majesty of the road they were following.

FIGURE 5.3. Students from The Ohio State University and other participants hike from the Hopeton site in Chillicothe to Newark along a conjectured path of the Great Hopewell Road. Remnants of the Hopeton Earthworks still visibly rise from the ground. Photo by Timothy E. Black.

My Hopewell Pilgrimage between Chillicothe and Newark

NORITA YODER

In my final quarter at The Ohio State University at Newark, I walked from the earthworks at Hopewell Culture National Historical Park in Chillicothe to the Octagon Earthworks in Newark as part of a course entitled "Earthworks Pilgrimage." It was one of my most memorable classes.

About thirty of us walked for seven days, tenting overnight, learning Ohio and Native history along the way. By the end of the week, we had walked approximately eighty miles, following as closely as possible the ancient route that archaeologist Brad Lepper has called the Great Hopewell Road. The experience allowed for a tiny glimpse into what ancient Indigenous people must have experienced in their close relationship with the natural world's rhythms and cycles.

As we walked, we learned about Ohio's ancient earthworks and gained a deep and personal respect for the land, for the Hopewell culture and for their earthworks. Chillicothe and Newark are home to the only octagonal earthworks ever built. Each octagon is connected to a circle, both of which are massive. Both align to the 18.6-year cycles of the moon. And both were built nearly 2,000 years ago using sophisticated geometry, astronomy, and engineering.

We also learned that visitors came to the Newark and Chillicothe earthwork sites from great distances across North America. These were ceremonial sites and very likely pilgrimage sites. Individually, the Hopewell Ceremonial Earthworks sites are worthy of UNESCO World Heritage status. The compelling evidence of their connectedness by a pilgrimage corridor or roadway bestows an even greater meaning on these sites.

As Dr. Lepper explains it, "This was like Jerusalem or Santiago de Compostela. It was a place where people came from miles around, like Mecca. It was a place of pilgrimage, and people were coming here bringing offerings, offerings of thanksgiving for healing, offerings in the hope of a blessing of some sort."

When something with the historical magnitude of the Hopewell Ceremonial Earthworks shifts our view such that, in the seeing, our individual place in history is shifted, it can deal a seismic shock to our individual identity. It is safe to say those who walked The Pilgrimage underwent a type of metamorphosis in those seven days.

As our group entered Newark on foot at the end of seven days and eighty miles, we had been changed. Our feet were sore, and some were limping, but we had gained a deep respect for the land we call Ohio. We were in awe of the ancient cultures who lived so closely attuned to the natural cycles that they built them into the land. In the remaking we found an abiding sense of our shared human experience, both past and present. It provided a surer footing and solid ground on which to walk forward, more whole, more confident in our own identity as part of greater humanity.

PART VI

Ancient Communities Coming Together

Behind the 7,000,000 cubic feet of earth that make up the Newark Complex are the people who carefully sculpted it 2,000 years ago. They had an inspiration. They had a vision. They had a commitment. The end result is still visible to us at Newark and the other sites of the Hopewell Ceremonial Earthworks nomination, but these earthen walls are not just a testament to the culture's achievement. They are also a testament to the people's dedication to one another and to later generations—including ours.

Indigenous Values Infuse the World Heritage Movement

CHRISTINE BALLENGEE MORRIS

Many years ago, when I was young, my parents would take me to mounds located in North Carolina and Virginia. Private places. Years later I would find myself in West Virginia, where there are mounds too. Public places. My relationship with the earthworks in Ohio began with the Great Circle (public place) and then proceeded to the Octagon Mound (private place for the chosen few). I became involved with an ad hoc group called Friends of the Mounds, and my research began to explore cultural sites that were either private or public.

My father, though not an enrolled tribal member, wanted us to know our Cherokee history and culture, which had not been easy for him since his mother passed away when he was young. People that I knew as relatives, who were friends of my grandmother, raised my father, and they became as well my family and cultural mentors. They emphasized Cherokee values. There are many Cherokee values, such as *gadugi,* a Cherokee word which means "coming together as one and helping one another," and *detsadaligenvdisgesdi,* "all must take responsibility for each other's well-being." The overarching themes I find in these values are respect and responsibility.

Cherokee values focus on one's responsibility to act communally and in a respectful way. As a researcher, honoring the core beliefs and values of an Indigenous community means to me creating a space where the gift of knowledge is acknowledged by giving back in some way to the individuals and community involved in the research. This coming together is *gadugi.* This is what I feel is happening now with the upcoming acknowledgment of Indigenous contributions in the status of World Heritage for the Ohio earthwork sites.

There are stories embedded in those earthworks, we just need to learn how to listen. Long before humanity had written language, we told our narratives through stories, poems, song, drawings, and dance. Stories not only convey information, but they have the power to change. The exchange of stories from teller to listener is a form of knowledge. As the story is consumed, the immediate reaction is heartfelt; then, as it proceeds to one's intellect, self-reflexive engagement occurs, which can lead to reimagining and maintaining relationships.

We all have many stories to share. We also have unique ways of viewing the world, which was affected by colonization, removal, and death. And yet, as Cherokee and other Indigenous people point out, We Are Still Here! I find the words from archaeologist Sonya Atalay (Anishinaabe-Ojibwe) to be insightful at this point: "Bringing Native voices to the foreground to share these experiences and worldviews is a critical part of readjusting the power balance to ensure that Native people control their own heritage, representation, and histories." World Heritage is a gift that I never thought I would see, but I am, and I am so thankful. So here is one more Cherokee word: *Wado* ("Thank you").

Licking County's 14,000-Year History

TIMOTHY R. W. JORDAN

Archaeologists date Indigenous people in Licking County back 14,000 years. Spearpoints shaped (or knapped) from Flint Ridge's Vanport flint provide one basis for this dating, but the flint was only one resource which brought the Paleoindian and Archaic people to this area.

The name we still use—Licking County—points toward another resource: salt deposits along the waterways. Indigenous people were long aware of this resource; the Licking River's Shawnee name is *Nepenime Sepe,* "Salt River." But more significant than the salt were the deer that it brought, and deer meant food, clothing, and other tools. To this day, hunters come to Licking County for trophy bucks. The huge racks these deer grow is a result of other minerals they lick up with the salt. For ancient people, deer antler was a preferred material for knapping flint-based tools.

This synergy of resources, along with fertile earth from Ohio's glacial period and numerous waterways for transporting people and resources, like the granite hammerstones used for quarrying flint, provided reasons for people to keep coming back to Licking County. But how could they make the area even more productive?

Pollen samples taken from the wall of the Great Circle show that the site was built on a prairie, not a forest as we expect from ancient Ohio. Controlled burning with fire would have cleared trees in a couple of ways. A burn would remove softer, faster-growing trees, leaving more room for hard-wooded oak, chestnut, walnut, and hickory—nut-producing trees. Removing the bark from these large hardwoods

so they would die and dry out (called girdling) would cause burning to clear everything. Grass, which is not plentiful in a forest, would then grow. With more grass to eat, the deer herds could reach larger sizes.

The results would have increased the area's food supply, creating an environment where people could stay longer. Adena burial mounds like the one at Dawes Arboretum, the Taft Reserve's Huffman Mound, and possibly the mounds next to Fairmount Presbyterian Church and at Infirmary Mound Park point to generations of people living out their lives in Licking County.

With the ability to stay close to this area, people could develop their culture and mythology in connection with it. During the Hopewell phenomenon, an artificial prairie would have been the perfect landscape on which to build the four-square-mile complex that is the Newark Earthworks. Nestled between Raccoon Creek, the South Fork of the Licking River, and Ramp Creek, this complex could easily be reached by people from all over the eastern half of North America, people who brought for trade or as offerings such exotic materials as the copper, mica, seashells, and obsidian found at the earthworks.

But the story of Native people in this area does not stop there. Later generations of the Fort Ancient Culture were also active here. Granville's Alligator Mound dates to this period. Probably not an actual alligator in Central Ohio, a better fit could be a mythological figure like the Underwater Panther, important to many Woodlands peoples. Perhaps it reflects later generations elaborating on the cosmological divisions between earth and a watery beneath world, which is also an interpretation of the Great Circle's moat or even the placement of the whole Newark Complex between its three waterways.

The petroglyph once at Black Hand Gorge perhaps dated to this period too. Positioned on the cliff face beneath Council Rock, where knappers worked flint quarried at Flint Ridge, the Black Hand provided a kind of signal to visitors paddling into the area along the Licking River.

Native people return to Licking County to this day. Their history surrounds the Newark Earthworks—and many other places—as we prepare for World Heritage recognition.

Building Earthworks, Building Community

JIM WILLIAMS

Have you ever stood outside at night and gazed up at the sky and wondered if anything—or anyone—is out there? Have you ever wondered if anyone is looking back at this blue marble and wondering about us?

I sometimes have, and a thousand different thoughts rush in on me. The things that felt so important before the sun went down suddenly seem smaller. I yearn for connection and significance. I want all of *this* to matter somehow in the vast universe. Somehow, I want the vast universe to connect to the ordinary and the orneriness of life around me.

Just maybe, an ancient visionary had the same thoughts and feelings, the same impulse to make connections beyond an individual lifespan and a single person, and even beyond the soil under their feet. Maybe they told a story, first in their own family and clan, and then beyond their intimate circle to those with whom they traded or intermarried.

I listened in fascination as a National Parks interpreter explained that the geometric earthworks built throughout Ohio could not have been completed by a small group of people. In order to accomplish this task, great bands of people had to come together. In the action of building these monumental earthworks, community was also built.

We don't know their story. We don't know their vision. All we have is what emerged from the community that grew from the story, inspired by the vision. It's written in soil and sweat, the stars above and the shape of the ground below. It wasn't built as we build today, with a contract and time frames and deadlines and down payments. It was built over more than one generation's lifespan. Somehow, the vision was caught by more than the net of one person's mystical night out with the stars and the moon.

Community brought the vision into reality. Working together, inspired by a vision of what could be, persons became a people and clan became community. They reached for something greater than the meaning and significance of one person and an idea. We don't really know what that vision was. We only know it must have been powerful and motivating because people traveled and gathered in order to be a part it.

It required mutual support, interactions, and shared experiences. Communication networks gathered people far and wide, but also translated the work from one generation to another. In soil and sweat, stars and water, the legacy is still spoken of from one generation to the next, and it creates community among us now.

Modern North American Tribes who have roots in the Ohio River Valley have taken the earthworks as a symbol of pride and banded together to preserve these sacred sites. Current residents of Ohio take the earthworks as a symbol of pride, as we recognize this marvel of the ancient world and band together as a community to preserve and share it with the world.

FIGURE 6.1. (*facing*) Mineral resources with distinctive origins outside of Licking County reflect the far-flung Hopewell Interaction Sphere. Pictured from the upper left are obsidian from Wyoming, a granite hammerstone carried south from Canada, Indiana hornstone, Arkansas novaculite, Coshocton chert, and pipestone from southern Ohio. Photo by Timothy E. Black.

FIGURE 6.2. Aerial photo of Alligator Mound. Its head is oriented uphill and its tail downhill to the left. Photo by Timothy E. Black.

A Prehistoric Legacy for the Present

RAY HIVELY AND ROBERT HORN

Two thousand years ago Indigenous people in Ohio developed over many generations a cultural record of achievement that is remarkable not only in the prehistory of North America but in all of prehistory. The Hopewell tradition is known for its sophisticated art, crafts, ritual, and widespread trade. Its greatest achievement, though, remains little known simply because of its monumental scale: built low to the ground over four miles, the Newark Earthworks are impossible to take in at a glance.

The design of the Earthworks is unique in its combination of size, geometrical precision, and astronomical knowledge—knowledge that could only be achieved after several generations of patient observing and careful recording of celestial events.

The various geometric figures at Newark and other Ohio Hopewell sites reveal the use of a standard unit of length (1,054 ft) and an ability to construct squares, circles, and octagons with closely equal areas. No other prehistoric culture is known to have achieved this level of geometric sophistication. The design, placement, and orientation of the earthworks integrate a deep Indigenous understanding of the local topography, the sky above, and geometrical knowledge. The extended massive walls of the linear figures define the most accurate astronomical alignments known in the prehistoric world.

The details of how and why these earthworks were constructed remain matters of continuing research, debate, and speculation. We can make some plausible inferences from their design. The monumental scale of the Newark Earthworks suggests that they were not built to impress a local audience with their size. Their precision and even their shapes are not visible from the ground. The oversized shapes are visible only from a vantage point high in the sky, inviting the "gods-eye" view of the sun and the moon. But the long sight lines to the horizon which these immense shapes define enabled the Hopewell-era designers to follow the celestial dance of sun and moon and perhaps to shape their ritual calendar according to its patterns.

In addition to the generations of observation and recording which made the earthworks possible, this magnificent feat of organization, design, and construction required the persistent effort of many laborers over many more generations. Yet it was all accomplished with no evidence of a centralized government, large population centers, military conquests, or slave labor. What kind of economic, social, and political structure could produce such great works? We can at least infer that such a system is possible. Current research is promising.

The decline and disappearance of the Hopewell tradition of monumental earthworks is another puzzle. Perhaps the failure of the sky gods to respond as hoped led to a gradual lessening of commitment and energy for the project. Perhaps the communities simply moved on to other priorities than monumental building.

Even if an intended message to the gods went unanswered, the earthworks then and today send a message to the rest of the world. It is a message of faith and hope in what people can accomplish when they are united by ideas of sufficient power to inspire their curiosity, creativity, imagination, and courage: a timeless legacy to the rest of the world.

FIGURE 6.3. (*facing*) Open house visitors getting a closer look at the Newark Octagon's artificial horizon. Photo by John E. Hancock.

92

A 2,000-Year-Old Intellectual Center

LUCY E. MURPHY

Two thousand years ago, scientists reported their findings in a place we now call Newark, Ohio. What they had learned was the result of interdisciplinary research, combining astronomy, mathematics, geography, civil engineering, landscape architecture, and, probably, theology. Like scholars today, the ancient scholars built upon the knowledge of previous generations of researchers. No doubt they shared the results of their studies orally, perhaps illustrating their talks with visual aids or site tours. Eventually, they recorded their knowledge on the land with the help of hundreds of volunteers in the creation of the massive Newark Earthworks.

It is likely that these earthworks were the brainchild of a charismatic visionary or small group of visionaries, but planning and creating this amazing project required the collaboration of myriad men and women with a variety of skills and understandings.

Originally, it seems, some people who were interested in the sun found places on the surrounding hilltops which corresponded with the solar equinoxes, places from which they had a good view of the valley below. Local residents, the heirs to generations of astronomers who had observed and recorded the moon's patterns over 18.6-year cycles, could share what they knew about the moon and its relationship to this place.

Teams of people signaling to each other between hilltops and valley floor plotted the locations of giant circles, octagon, and square. Experts who had built earthworks elsewhere brought the skills and traditions of mound building to this place, including a sophisticated understanding of geometry and standard units of measurement. This would also have included the knowledge of how to recruit and inspire people to dedicate some of their time and energy, and to organize their efforts to move an estimated 7,000,000 cubic feet of dirt one basket at a time.

While the earthworks were being created, and afterwards, visitors came to this place for ceremonies, festivals, rituals, and trade, but many also probably came to learn skills, to gain knowledge, and to share their own ideas and knowledge with others.

I am a history professor, researcher, and author, and when I visit and ponder the Newark Earthworks, I recognize this place as an ancient intellectual center whose leaders, creators, and visitors were remarkably similar to the scholars, scientists, artists, professors, innovators, and students at today's universities, research centers, and think tanks. Nowadays, scholars present the results of our research as lectures and other oral presentations to gatherings of interested listeners in classrooms and conferences, by writing articles and books, and sometimes with visual displays of posters, websites, performances, museum exhibits, and signage in significant places. In religiously affiliated colleges, scholars and their neighbors offer prayers and participate in ceremonies and rituals in chapels and other sacred spaces.

The ancient researchers may not have written books that we know of, but otherwise, their activities closely mirrored those of present-day scholars, academics, and thought leaders. Their findings were expressed in these extraordinary mounds and related activities. To my mind, the Newark Earthworks site was not only a place of great ceremony, but also an important center of research, learning, and teaching.

FIGURE 7.1. (*following*) Tour group walking the passageway connecting the Octagon to its Observatory Circle. Photo by Timothy E. Black.

PART VII

Modern Communities Coming Together

Today, the example of ancestral Indigenous people can provide a mirror for us as their earthworks continue to pull people together. Working for World Heritage recognition has brought together modern Indigenous peoples and archaeologists; historians and other scholars; Ohio History Connection administrators and county officials; interpreters and local stakeholders. These partnerships have been forged both within and across Licking, Ross, and Warren Counties. And beyond that, the Hopewell Ceremonial Earthworks draw in visitors from across Ohio, America, and, indeed, the world.

Growing Up in the Mahoning Valley

JAY TOTH

In the 1950s, the removal of an Indian burial mound near Youngstown, Ohio attracted a lot of public interest. As a five-year-old, I asked, "Why? How could someone dig up the dead simply because they did not want them on their property? Why did no one stop it?"

I grew up in the Mahoning Valley in a community of Native families relocated by the Indian Relocation Act of 1956. As a child, I did not know that this was a government assimilation effort—it was just my neighborhood, and in it I was exposed to many viewpoints on tribal and non-tribal issues. On occasion, the mothers of the community would meet in the front yards to talk. I once overheard them wondering why the Oklahoma Cherokee family always flew the American flag.

Eventually, we moved. I entered a new, racially and economically diverse school where black kids, white kids, poor kids, and rich kids all got along—we were all members of the Tiger clan. It was 1967, and Ohio had recently passed legislation requiring a state history component in the middle school curriculum. I remember noticing that there were only a few pages on Ohio Indians. The book briefly covered tribes of the historic period, but there was no mention of earthworks or prehistory. Our class frequently omitted the history and culture of Natives.

I went to college at Youngstown State University and was fortunate to study anthropology under Dr. John White, who brought a new perspective to archaeology. Instead of focusing on treasure hunting and artifact collecting, he promoted site preservation. For this he was ridiculed by traditional mainstream archaeologists of the 1970s. In that period the prevailing American view was that Native cultural sites had little value. These sentiments persist to this day. John, however, believed Native sites like the Newark and Serpent Mound earthworks were just as important as other internationally recognized sites of antiquity. He knew, though, that ethnocentrism and political opinions would impede the preservation of Native sites in the state. He was right: there is still no legislation prohibiting the desecration of mounds and earthworks in Ohio.

My background and training ultimately led to invaluable experiences in Native and non-Native communities across the country. Over the years I have seen progress in Indian affairs, government-to-government relations, and an increase in public sensitivity toward Native concerns, but at both the federal and state levels, embedded discriminatory views on all things Indian remain. Changes in perspective and politics have happened slowly. In recent years, state organizations like the Ohio History Connection have taken a leading role in recognizing the significance and sacredness of Native sites. Open dialogue with Ohio's Tribal Nations is encouraged and valued. As welcoming, cooperative relationships have developed, Ohio's Indigenous people have been given a voice that had been silenced far too long.

The progress we are collectively making is evident in the nomination of designated Ohio earthworks, including those in Newark, as UNESCO World Heritage Sites. These sacred places can be preserved for future generations and appreciated as they ought to be. Ohio's Native earthworks can take their place among all the other awe-inspiring World Heritage Sites. This is exactly what John White had envisioned.

Seeing the Moon Again for the First Time

JEFF GILL

Learning about the Newark Earthworks and sharing their story with new audiences over the last thirty years, I've become aware of a few things.

One, of course, is how many people know little or nothing about what Native people accomplished on this continent 2,000 years ago. People who are aware of all sorts of details about kings and queens and pharaohs, pyramids and Stonehenge and cathedrals, even though they've never been outside of this country, are at best dimly aware of "mounds."

And I've been in conversations where people speak excitedly of a European trip where they rented a room for a week on a square "right across from a church that's a thousand years old!" If I reply, "Did you know every time you drive down 30th Street in Newark you're in the middle of an earthwork complex that's twice that age," it's likely to be met with initial disbelief.

I enjoy teaching people, both local residents and international visitors, old and young, about this gem of prehistory and culture we have in our midst—but I also value what I've learned myself. One big part of that learning has been about the moon.

Sure, I knew there was a moon in the sky, and I'm old enough to have followed the Apollo program mission by mission with great excitement; I can still tell you where on the visible surface on a full moon night you could spot the Sea of Tranquility.

The Old Farmer's Almanac had helped me be dimly aware of the phases, waxing gibbous and waning crescent and so on, cycling from sliver to bright round rise at the full, opposite the sunset. What I wasn't really conscious of, though, until I came to become acquainted with the Newark Earthworks, was how the moon's arc can swing from high in the sky to low on the southern horizon: not within the course of a year, as the sun's path runs, but within weeks.

Even as I know the sun's time in the sky at our latitude gets shorter each day to the winter solstice, then from December 21 longer each day as the path overhead gets consistently higher, until the summer solstice in June, I had not noticed how the moon's rise and set cycles on a different pattern altogether, in the sky during the day at times, rising nearly an hour later each night, more or less, shifting north and south in its westward path overhead.

Now, after delving deep into what's known and what we still struggle to understand about the geometry and astronomy of the Octagon portion of the Newark Earthworks, I find that somewhere in the back of my head I'm more aware of the moon than I once was. I step outside and look up, anticipating the moon's presence and place in the sky, and there it is. The moon used to surprise me, but now it's more of a constant companion, anticipated and welcomed in its natural place in the sky.

Something like the components of an analog clock, the sun is the easy-to-notice second hand of the cosmos we live in, the seasons are the minute hand, and the moon, perhaps, the hour. Once you understand a bit more deeply how the whole system works, the parts and their movements make more sense, and even start to find echoes inside your own awareness.

FIGURE 7.2. Time-lapse photo showing the minimum southern moonset at the Octagon. Although one of the Octagon's walls again forms a sightline, the lunar alignment occurs just before the moon disappears rather than when it first breaks the artificial horizon. Photo by Timothy E. Black.

Want a Better Community? Be Awestruck

M. ELIZABETH WEISER

As a rhetorician, I study how our communal identity is formed and how that identity affects our communal actions. So, when I read about the power of *awe* recently, I immediately thought about how it could help our community. Awe shows why it's important to understand what a special piece of ground we inhabit here, surrounding the Newark Earthworks.

Psychologists find that feelings of awe make us better community members. By *awe* they mean the feeling that something is vast, either in physical size (like a beautiful landscape) or in intellectual size (like a mind-blowing concept). That vastness has to challenge our current understanding of the world, they say. You have to be a bit awestruck in the face of the sublime.

Experiencing awe, in turn, leads to feeling humbler, having greater feelings of happiness and well-being. Awe-inspired people are more generous and make more ethical decisions. They are better community members. "When personal concerns and goals appear less important, attention gets directed to the greater society," says Galadriel Watson, author of the article.

The more we interpret the Newark Earthworks, the more awe-inspiring they are. But it's not just the earthworks themselves—it's the whole valley we live in. To the ancients, our whole area was infused with awe-inspiring wonders. According to calculations by Ray Hively and Robert Horn, the hills and valleys of Newark and Heath were part of a cosmological map that allowed ancient people to attempt through their earthen constructions to unify sky, earth, and the community that lived between them.

We should all be familiar by now with Hively and Horn's discovery that the Octagon Earthworks was built to precisely track the moon. But they argue for an even more vast cosmology. Their research finds that from the four nearest prominent hilltops surrounding our valley, sightlines marking the precise locations of the four most important moonrise architectural features of both the Octagon and Great Circle are easily traced. And here's where the awe comes in: lines between these four points also accurately mark the path of the sun on its summer and winter solstices. Observing the sky from the highest point of the Newark area, Coffman's Knob, yields further cosmological sightlines—all converging on the floor of the valley in the exact locations where people came together over multiple generations to observe, measure, and build this complex of monumental structures.

To the people living during the Hopewell era, our valley would have seemed a giant cosmological miracle, to which they added their own architectural structures to highlight it. It would be as if Bethlehem still had its star shining directly over it. No other site anywhere approaches this vast convergence—and the response of the people was awe. What practical reason could there be for this monumental construction, Hively and Horn ask, but "reverence, awe, recognition of mystery, and fear of the cosmic power" in a landscape where people lived close to the earth and continually under the sky.

So, stop and look up at the hills around us. Imagine generations of people making detailed observations to mark places—perhaps where you are standing right now—that would have engendered such awe that they spent lifetimes building with neighbors and strangers, much as medieval communities spent lifetimes building cathedrals. Ask yourself what it's like to live in what 2,000 years ago was Jerusalem or Mecca.

And then look around at the community and let yourself feel a bit more of the awestruck humility, the generous communality, which might come from standing on holy ground.

"I don't think we need to be climbing mountains in order to experience awe. I think it's closer to home than we realize," says psychology researcher David Yaden. In fact, here in Newark it might be literally right in our backyard, if we let ourselves notice it.

Drawn Together at Earthworks

TIMOTHY R. W. JORDAN

Since 2013, I've been one of the interpreters to greet people as they visited the Newark Earthworks sites. Many have been Ohioans, coming from Columbus and other parts of the state, but I've met guests from New York, Florida, Texas, California, Washington, and many places in between. In the last few years, the sites have increasingly become truly international, with visitors coming from England, Germany, Latvia, India, China, and Japan, just to name a few.

The Newark Earthworks and other Native earthworks sites in our World Heritage nomination have drawn people from across the known world for thousands of years. We find at earthworks sites copper from Lake Superior, mica from the Appalachian Mountains, seashells from the Gulf of Mexico, and obsidian from Yellowstone National Park. All had to be brought here. Going out from Licking County was the blood red-, turquoise-, and aquamarine-colored flint from Flint Ridge. Perhaps this exchange was trade, or perhaps this movement of exotic and beautiful materials was part of the ceremonies that brought people together here.

What kinds of ceremonies?

In 2015, I was part of the group who watched the cluster of lunar alignments built into the Octagon at the midpoint of the moon's 18.6-year cycle. Gathering in darkness, we waited for the moon's white glow to appear at the far end of the wall we sighted along. Sometimes as an orb, other times as only a crescent, the moon would slowly appear. It crept across the sky, almost imperceptible in its movements if not for its position relative to the end of the earthwork wall or a nearby tree branch. The higher it rose, the whiter and purer its light became.

We can't know what kinds of stories ancient people told as part of the ceremonies at the Octagon and other earthworks sites, but today's Indigenous people—the descendants of the builders—have sometimes shared stories with us. One story, a version of which appears on the website ancientohiotrail.org, speaks of Grandmother Moon. It emphasizes the relationship between older and younger generations and ends with the departure of the grandmother with the promise that she will continue to watch over her grandchildren from the moon.

Such a theme of looking to the moon to remember ancestors overlaps well with the mechanics of the Octagon's alignments and the experience of watching a moonrise. For me, watching the moon's gentle progress across the sky was a chance to reflect on the passage of time. I thought how I will look forward to witnessing the alignments with my three nephews in 2025 and 2034. I thought of deceased relatives I would have loved to show the alignments to. One evening in 2015, a close friend joined me for watching the moonrise. In the last few years, he has passed away, so in the future watching the moon will be a way to remember him.

I grew up in Licking County and returned to it ten years ago. I've benefited firsthand from the value our local communities place on being kind and welcoming. Sharing the Newark Earthworks with the rest of the world is perfectly in keeping with this value.

It's what the people did in this area 2,000 years ago.

Universal Value and Significance

HOPE TAFT

When I was First Lady of Ohio, I had the privilege of coming to Newark and Licking County many times to enjoy and participate in your most exciting tourist attractions. I still like to come to Dawes Arboretum and look at the tree that my husband Bob planted there. One of our Christmas card photos was taken in the Black Hand Gorge. The Works museum brought early settler life in Ohio alive to the young folks I had in tow. I was thrilled when a fourth-grade class learned about How a Bill Becomes a Law and made the Newark Earthworks Ohio's official prehistoric monument. We hung a print of the Octagon Earthworks on the Governor's Residence wall honoring this occasion.

But perhaps the most exciting visit was the evening we were invited to watch the moonrise over the Octagon. I will never forget seeing that illuminated ball rise through the gaps as it has done for 2,000 years. I am still in awe of the Indigenous people who figured out how to do this when 18.6 years pass between two extreme northernmost moonrises, but the average age of a male was just thirty-five years old. Then consider the organizational skills needed to build mounds fourteen feet high, one basket-load at a time, into perfect geometric designs at one time covering more than four square miles. Moving 7,000,000 cubic feet of earth was a cooperative effort of people who lived in small family groups growing and gathering their own food. Yet they made the time to build these monumental structures. Similar earthwork designs in similar sizes are found in Chillicothe, seventy miles away. Many more were in Ohio before the settlers came. One can still be seen rising toward the sky on the Dawes Arboretum property.

Yet to be clearly defined is the importance of Ohio flint from Flint Ridge, just east of Newark, to this civilization. Bits of it are found all over what is now the United States. Does that suggest that these people traveled and traded with others as far away as the Rocky Mountains, the Atlantic Coast, and Canada? Or does it suggest that Newark was a ceremonial site that visitors periodically came to and then took a bit of flint home with them as a reminder of a profound experience? There is still a lot to learn about these remarkable people, but what is known can be found on the websites ancientohiotrail.org and world-heritageohio.org.

Licking County's treasures as well as Hopewell sites in Chillicothe and at Fort Ancient are up for UNESCO World Heritage Site designation because they have universal value and significance. That nighttime visit to Newark has compelled me to work for their inclusion in this worldwide list of must-see places. There is no better place to see ancient earthworks from this time period than in Ohio.

I hope you will embrace this opportunity to learn more about these Ancient Ohioans and work to make their heritage known worldwide. It will put Newark, Licking County, and Ohio on a very special list of a thousand "must see" places in the world.

FIGURE 7.3. (*facing*) The colors and patterns in Flint Ridge's Vanport flint. Photo by Timothy E. Black.

A World Heritage Fledgling

JENNIFER AULTMAN

Soon, the world will know that 2,000 years ago Indigenous people in the land now called Licking County developed a cultural tradition significant in human history. As I write this, the UNESCO World Heritage Centre in Paris is reviewing copies of the Hopewell Ceremonial Earthworks World Heritage nomination, comprising the Octagon and Great Circle Earthworks in Licking County, five sites at Hopewell Culture National Historical Park in Chillicothe, and Fort Ancient in Warren County. I can hardly believe that the application is finished and submitted! In order to show how significant this milestone is, I want to share an insider's view, as the OHC's World Heritage project director, on this World Heritage journey.

Nearly twenty years ago, a small group of experts from Ohio History Connection, the National Park Service, The Ohio State University at Newark, and other organizations concluded that Ohio's Indigenous earthworks belong on the World Heritage List with places like Notre Dame cathedral, Rapa Nui (Easter Island), and Stonehenge. This team had studied and visited World Heritage Sites around the globe and was convinced that the earthworks were just as significant.

Fast forward twenty years. In 2018–2021, our team of writers and researchers worked diligently to prepare the final World Heritage nomination dossier for the Hopewell Ceremonial Earthworks. At least ten writers and editors, two graphic designers, one mapmaker, several reviewers, and many supporting team members crafted a 332-page document that details exactly how these eight earthworks exhibit World Heritage-level Outstanding Universal Value. We compiled thousands of pages of supporting documents—from protective laws to the level of threat posed by natural disasters, to the types of programs and facilities at each site.

In long-term projects, a shocking moment can happen when the project flies on its own. For me, that moment came on December 31, 2021. I had worked through the holidays making sure that the application package met every single requirement—that no files were inadvertently forgotten, no USB drives malfunctioned, no technicality missed that could sink the effort. With everything meticulously packed up, my husband and I made the trip to the FedEx facility in Columbus. Barely breathing, I handed the boxes over. They disappeared into the abyss, headed to the National Park Service Office of International Affairs in Washington, DC. It was like sending my child off to the first day of college, knowing I had to trust a series of others to help them make the rest of the journey on their own.

We depended on the Park Service to pass the package on to the US State Department. The State Department, in turn, hand-delivered the package to the UNESCO World Heritage Centre in Paris. What a thrill it was when we got the news that this handoff was done! And then came the next milestone: the first level of review determined that the nomination is technically complete! More reviews will continue through 2022. We anticipate that in the summer of 2023 the World Heritage Committee will inscribe these eight Hopewell Ceremonial Earthworks onto the World Heritage List. And that will be only the beginning.

Above all, the project team seeks to honor the achievements of the

Native people who lived here 2,000 years ago. As Marti Chaatsmith, associate director of the Newark Earthworks Center at Ohio State Newark and a citizen of the Comanche Nation, has beautifully written, "Gathering up specific kinds of earth and precisely forming them into geometric shapes in a planned and purposeful way was an act of gathering power." The earthworks are powerful places, and now the world will know it.

FIGURE 7.4. (*following*) Archaeology students from the University of Toronto visiting the Great Circle. They represent a small part of the growing international interest in the Newark Earthworks. Photo by Timothy E. Black.

109

Acknowledgments

We would like to thank the following generous donors and supporters for their efforts in the publication of this book:

Anonymous

Licking County Foundation

Newark Advocate

The Ohio State University College of Arts and Sciences

The Ohio State University Department of English

The Ohio State University Department of History

The Ohio State University at Newark Cultural Arts and Events
    Committee

The Ohio State University at Newark Office of the Dean/Director

The Ohio State University at Newark Office of Outreach and
    Engagement

We also gratefully acknowledge all the writers and photographers who donated their creative time and talent—and those in particular who provided permission for the images in this book:

Timothy E. Black

John E. Hancock

Brad Lepper

Ohio History Connection

Contributors

JENNIFER AULTMAN is the project director for World Heritage at the Ohio History Connection.

CHRISTINE BALLENGEE MORRIS, of Cherokee and Appalachian ancestry, was on the World Heritage Ohio Steering Committee's American Indian Work Group. A National Art Education Association Fellow, she is a professor of arts administration, education, and policy at The Ohio State University, where she directs American Indian studies.

TIMOTHY E. BLACK is a retired news photographer and editor who has been photographing Ohio's ancient sites for the Newark Earthworks Center since 2006.

MARY F. BORGIA is a gifted intervention specialist with the Newark City Schools.

MARTI L. CHAATSMITH is an enrolled citizen of the Comanche Nation and direct descendant of the Choctaw Nation of Oklahoma, the associate director of the Newark Earthworks Center, and a World Heritage Ohio Ambassador.

JEFF GILL is a World Heritage Ohio Ambassador who has given tours of the earthworks to thousands of people.

STACEY HALFMOON is Choctaw, Delaware, and an enrolled citizen of the Caddo Nation who is senior director of the Choctaw Cultural Center.

JOHN E. HANCOCK is an emeritus professor of architecture at the University of Cincinnati and principal author of the Hopewell Ceremonial Earthworks World Heritage nomination.

RAY HIVELY is an emeritus professor of physics and astronomy at Earlham College in Richmond, Indiana.

ROBERT HORN is an emeritus professor of philosophy at Earlham College in Richmond, Indiana.

TIMOTHY R. W. JORDAN worked as an interpreter and site manager for the Newark Earthworks and Flint Ridge Ancient Quarries and Nature Preserve from 2013 to 2022. He is on the English faculty of Zane State College and is a seminarian at Trinity Lutheran Seminary.

AARON KEIRNS is the author of *Black Hand Gorge: An Illustrated Guide* and several other books on Ohio history topics.

BRAD LEPPER is the senior archaeologist for the Ohio History Connection's World Heritage Program. His research has focused on the Hopewell culture and especially on the Newark Earthworks.

JOHN N. LOW, an associate professor at The Ohio State University and the director of the Newark Earthworks Center, is a citizen of the Pokagon Band of the Potawatomi Indian nation of southwest Michigan/northwest Indiana.

MIKE MICKELSON is an emeritus professor of physics and astronomy at Denison University.

LUCY E. MURPHY is an emeritus professor of history at The Ohio State University, specializing in intercultural, interracial, and gender relations on Midwestern American borderlands.

BRET J. RUBY is an archeologist with the National Park Service and Chief of Resource Management at Hopewell Culture National Historical Park in Chillicothe, Ohio.

RICHARD D. SHIELS is an emeritus associate professor of history at The Ohio State University and the founding director of the university's Newark Earthworks Center.

HOPE TAFT, the First Lady of Ohio from 1999 to 2007, is a World Heritage Ohio volunteer ambassador who has organized multiple tours and events at Ohio's Indigenous sites.

JAY TOTH was a tribal archaeologist for the Ho-chunk and Seneca Nations. Retired, he now lives on the Allegany Reservation.

GLENNA J. WALLACE is the Chief of the Eastern Shawnee Tribe of Oklahoma and a former professor and administrator at Crowder College in Missouri.

BILL WEAVER served on the World Heritage Ohio Steering Committee.

M. ELIZABETH WEISER is a professor of rhetoric and museology in the Department of English at The Ohio State University, specializing in public memory and national narratives.

JIM WILLIAMS is a certified interpretive guide at the Great Circle and the program coordinator for Flint Ridge Historic Quarries and Nature Preserve.

NORITA YODER is the president of the Zollikon Institute, an educational initiative serving Ohio's Amish and Mennonite populations, located in Berlin, Ohio.